"Whenever my friend David ~~ships, I listen. Far from disp~~ anchors from Scripture and b~~ practical steps in embracing tl~~ the book on suffering. David's _____ ___ ___ _____ me through a significant portion of my years as a quadriplegic, and I highly commend *God's Grace in Your Suffering*. What a great guide for those who, every day, journey the hard, bloodstained path to Calvary."

Joni Eareckson Tada, Founder, Joni and Friends International Disability Center

"Sometimes navigating the advice of others while in the midst of suffering can be an added trial. Powlison puts all of that to rest by giving readers the gospel—showing them the firm foundation of the Word. He puts the compass of God's Word in our trembling hands and points us to true north: Christ himself."

Gloria Furman, coeditor, *Word-Filled Women's Ministry*; author, *The Pastor's Wife*

"Tender, refreshing, and thoroughly biblical, *God's Grace in Your Suffering* is a cup of cold water for those in the desert of suffering. Writing from the perspective of both a fellow sufferer and a wise counselor, Powlison gently leads us to find God's goodness, grace, and comforting presence in our pain. We see how God is at work in our trials and can bring gold out of our afflictions. My copy is well marked as I know I will refer to this insightful book again and again!"

Vaneetha Rendall Risner, author, *The Scars That Have Shaped Me: How God Meets Us in Suffering*

"Because David Powlison understands that 'profound good in our lives often emerges in a crucible of significant suffering,' he is fit to lead us in a workshop on suffering and God's grace. And that's exactly what *God's Grace in Your Suffering* is—a workshop where Powlison walks us through Scripture, the hymn 'How Firm a Foundation,' and our (and his) experiences, that we may see God's goodness and seek God's grace in and through our suffering."

Juan R. Sanchez, Senior Pastor, High Pointe Baptist Church, Austin, Texas; author, *1 Peter for You* and *Seven Dangers Facing Your Church*

"Here's a short book that is long on biblical wisdom for real life. I look forward to putting this book into the hands of those who struggle to connect the promises of the Bible with the painful realities of life in this world in a way that brings peace."

Nancy Guthrie, author, *Hearing Jesus Speak into Your Sorrow*

"Yes and amen! David Powlison brings together suffering and the powerful, tender God who is with us in our sufferings and in whom they have meaning and purpose. You will find a big-picture view that breathes hope and encouragement, as well as profound nuggets that you will want to tape up over the kitchen sink to savor. As always, David makes things practical, personal, and 'ordinary.' If you live in this broken world, you will want to read this book!"

Elizabeth W. D. Groves, Lecturer in Old Testament, Westminster Theological Seminary; author, *Grief Undone* and *Becoming a Widow*

GOD'S GRACE
IN YOUR
SUFFERING

Other Crossway Books by David Powlison

How Does Sanctification Work?

Making All Things New: Restoring Joy to the Sexually Broken

GOD'S GRACE
IN YOUR
SUFFERING

DAVID POWLISON

WHEATON, ILLINOIS

God's Grace in Your Suffering

Copyright © 2018 by David Powlison

Published by Crossway
        1300 Crescent Street
        Wheaton, Illinois 60187

All rights reserved. No part of this publication may be reproduced, stored in a retrieval system, or transmitted in any form by any means, electronic, mechanical, photocopy, recording, or otherwise, without the prior permission of the publisher, except as provided for by USA copyright law. Crossway® is a registered trademark in the United States of America.

Cover image and design: Jordan Singer

First printing 2018

Printed in the United States of America

Unless otherwise indicated, Scripture quotations are from the ESV® Bible (The Holy Bible, English Standard Version®), copyright © 2001 by Crossway, a publishing ministry of Good News Publishers. Used by permission. All rights reserved.

Scripture quotations marked NASB are from The New American Standard Bible®. Copyright © The Lockman Foundation 1960, 1962, 1963, 1968, 1971, 1972, 1973, 1975, 1977, 1995. Used by permission.

Scripture references marked NIV are taken from The Holy Bible, New International Version®, NIV®. Copyright © 1973, 1978, 1984, 2011 by Biblica, Inc.™ Used by permission. All rights reserved worldwide.

Trade paperback ISBN: 978-1-4335-5618-0
ePub ISBN: 978-1-4335-5621-0
PDF ISBN: 978-1-4335-5619-7
Mobipocket ISBN: 978-1-4335-5620-3

Library of Congress Cataloging-in-Publication Data

Names: Powlison, David, 1949– author.
Title: God's grace in your suffering / David Powlison.
Description: Wheaton: Crossway, 2018. | Includes bibliographical references and index.
Identifiers: LCCN 2017017293 (print) | LCCN 2017052509 (ebook) | ISBN 9781433556197 (pdf) | ISBN 9781433556203 (mobi) | ISBN 9781433556210 (epub) | ISBN 9781433556180 (tp)
Subjects: LCSH: How firm a foundation. | Hymns, English—History and criticism. | Consolation. | Suffering—Religious aspects—Christianity.
Classification: LCC BV317.H69 (ebook) | LCC BV317.H69 P69 2018 (print) | DDC 248.8/6—dc23
LC record available at https://lccn.loc.gov/2017017293

Crossway is a publishing ministry of Good News Publishers.

LB		28	27	26	25	24	23	22	21	20	19	18
15	14	13	12	11	10	9	8	7	6	5	4	3	2	1

To the men and women
with whom I am privileged to work at the
Christian Counseling & Educational Foundation.
Your faith, love, wisdom, and gifts mean so much to
me personally. You give riches to the body of Christ.
You give your very selves. Thank you.

We most humbly beseech thee, of thy goodness, O Lord, to comfort and succor all those who, in this transitory life, are in trouble, sorrow, need, sickness, or any other adversity.

Book of Common Prayer

———

Blessed be the God and Father of our Lord Jesus Christ, the Father of mercies and God of all comfort, who comforts us in all our affliction, so that we may be able to comfort those who are in any affliction, with the comfort with which we ourselves are comforted by God.

2 Corinthians 1:3–4

CONTENTS

INTRODUCTION

Job, his wife, and his three friends agreed on two things. Our lives are "few of days and full of trouble" (Job 14:1), and God's hand is intimately mixed up in our troubles. But strife and perplexity set in among them when they tried to explain exactly how God and troubles connect.

They argued about the cause of Job's troubles; no one understood the backstory of cosmic drama. They argued about what God was up to; no one understood that God had purposes for good beyond human comprehension and he was not punishing Job. They argued about the validity of Job's professed faith and faithfulness; no one understood that Job was both the genuine article and a work in progress. And they argued about *who* needed to do *what* in response to affliction; no one understood that the Lord would show up, that he would be asking the questions, that his purposes would be fulfilled. The Lord himself described Job as "a blameless and upright man, who fears God and turns away from evil" (Job 1:8). But who could have predicted the tumultuous journey that proved that fact?

Thousands of years later, we humankind are still short-lived and still much afflicted. And our troubles still perplex us. Why is this happening to me? Where is God? What is he doing? What does faith look like? How does the Lord show up? Why is the journey so tumultuous?

And what difference does it make that in between Job's afflictions back then and your afflictions right now, the Word became flesh and dwelt among us? Job said:

> I know that my Redeemer lives,
>> and at the last he will stand upon the earth.
> And after my skin has been thus destroyed,
>> yet in my flesh I shall see God,
> whom I shall see for myself,
>> and my eyes shall behold, and not another.
>> My heart faints within me! (Job 19:25–27)

Job's Redeemer came to him at last. The Lord answered out of the whirlwind, and Job said, "Now my eye sees you" (Job 42:5). But we see even more clearly. From where we stand, we see Jesus Christ. We see more of who the Redeemer is. We see more of how he did it. We say more than Job could say: "God, who said, 'Let light shine out of darkness,' has shone in our hearts to give the light of the knowledge of the glory of God in the face of Jesus Christ" (2 Cor. 4:6). We see. But our lives are still "few of days and full of trouble."

Here is the central concern of the book before you. When you face trouble, loss, disability, and pain, *how* does the God and Father of our Lord Jesus Christ meet you and comfort you? How does grace and goodness find you, touch you, work with you, and walk with you through deep waters? You probably already know something of the "right answer." Consider three sweeping truths.

First, it is obvious from both Scripture and experience that God *never* establishes a no-fly zone keeping all problems away. He never promises that your life will be safe, easy, peaceful, healthy, and prosperous. On the contrary, you and I are certain to experience danger, hardship, turmoil, ill health, and loss. And some of God's beloved children live lives particularly fraught with physical pain, poverty, isolation, betrayal, and loss. For all of us, death is the inevitable and impending final affliction. We humankind are mariposa lilies in Death Valley after rain. We flourish for a moment. Then the wind passes over us, and we are gone, and no trace remains. That's the description of God's blessed and beloved children according to Psalm 103:15–16. And, of course, people who are estranged from God also live brief and troubled lives. We cannot read God's favor or disfavor by assessing how troubled a person's life is.

Second, it is obvious from Scripture and experience that we also sample joys and good gifts from God's hand. The mariposa lily is beautiful in its season. Most people taste something of what is good—familial care perhaps, and daily bread, occasional feasting, a measure of good health, friends and companions, moments of beauty, opportunity to become good at something, committed love, children's laughter, a job well done, the innocent pleasure of resting after working, and perhaps a restful sleep. There are no guarantees of any particular earthly good, but all good gifts may be gratefully enjoyed.

Some people seem unusually blessed with temporal joys. Job enjoyed unusually good gifts at both the beginning and the end of his life—Satan had accused the Lord of giving Job a cushy life as a bribe for faith. And arrogant people, at odds with God and self-reliant, may also enjoy an easy life of good health, growing wealth, and the admiration of others. That's how Psalm 73:3–12 describes people who flourish though they deem the Lord irrelevant. We cannot read God's favor or disfavor by assessing how easy and trouble-free a person's life is.

Third, it's obvious from Scripture—and it can become deeply rooted in experience—that God speaks and acts through affliction. As C. S. Lewis says, "God whispers to us in our pleasures, speaks in our conscience, but shouts in our pain: it is His megaphone to rouse a deaf world."[1] The purpose of this book is to anchor your experience more deeply in God's goodness. Suffering reveals the genuineness of faith in Christ. And suffering produces genuine faith. For example, when you struggle under affliction, the Psalms become real. True faith deepens, brightens, and grows wise. You grow up in knowing God. When you are the genuine article, you are also and always a work in progress.

Suffering is both the acid test and the catalyst. It reveals and forms faith. It also exposes and destroys counterfeit faith. Afflictions expose illusory hopes invested in imaginary gods. Such disillusionment is a good thing, a severe mercy. The destruction of what is false invites repentance and faith in God as he truly is. Suffering brings a foretaste of the loss of every good thing for those who profess no faith in the one Savior of the world, God's inexpressible gift, the Lifegiver. Affliction presses on unbelief. It presses unbelief toward bitterness, or despair, or addiction, or ever more desperate illusions, or ever more deadly self-satisfaction—or to a reconsideration of what lasts. To lose what you are living for, when those treasures are vanities, invites comprehensive repentance. We can read God's favor or disfavor by noticing how a person responds to affliction.

God's hand is intimately mixed up in our troubles. Each day will bring you "its own trouble" (Matt. 6:34). Some difficulties are light and momentary—in your face today and forgotten tomorrow. Other hardships last for a season. Some troubles recur and abate cyclically. Other afflictions become chronic. Some woes steadily worsen, progressively bringing pain and disability into your life. And other sufferings arrive with inescapable finality—the death of a dream, the death of a loved one, your own dying and death. But whatever you must face changes in light of the resurrection of Jesus Christ and the promise that you, too, will live. Faith can grow up. You can learn to say with all your heart, in company with a great cloud of witnesses: "We do not lose heart. Though our outer self is wasting away, our inner self is being renewed day by day. For this light momentary affliction is preparing for us an eternal weight of glory beyond all comparison" (2 Cor. 4:16–17). We can learn to say it and mean it, because it is true.

If you are someone who has taken the book of Psalms to heart, if you've pondered the second half of Romans 8, if you've worked your way through Job, if you've let 1 Peter sink in, then you've already got the gist of how God's grace works in hardships. But there are always new challenges. The wisdom to suffer well is like manna—you must receive nourishment every day. You can't store it up, though you do become more familiar with how to go out and find what you need for today.

How will God actually engage *your* sufferings with his grace? You may know the right answer in theory. You may have known it firsthand in some difficult situations. And yet you'll find that you don't know God well enough or in the exact ways you need to for the next thing that comes your way.

We take God's hard answer and make it sound like a pat answer. He sets about a long slow answer*ing*, but we're after a quick fix. His answer insists on being lived out over time and into the particulars. We act as if just saying the right words makes it so. God's answer involves changing you into a different kind of person. But we act as if some truth, principle, strategy, or perspective might simply be incorporated into who we already are. God personalizes his answer on hearts with an uncanny flexibility. But we turn it into a formula: "If you just believe x. If you just do y. If you just remember z." No important truth ever contains the word "just" in the punch line.

We can make the right answer sound old hat, but I guarantee this: God will surprise you. He will make you stop. You will struggle. He will bring you up short. You will hurt. He will take his time. You will grow in faith and in love. He will deeply delight you. You will find the process harder than you ever imagined—and better. Goodness and mercy will follow you all the days of your life. At the end of the long road you will come home at last. No matter how many times you've heard it, no matter how long you've known it, no matter how well you can say it, God's answer will come to mean something better than you could ever imagine.

He answers with himself.[2]

1

YOUR SIGNIFICANT

SUFFERING

Think of this book as a workshop. Put yourself into the story and you will get more out of it. Scripture is custom-designed to engage any and all difficulties we face in life. So put your troubles on the table. Listen to how our Lord invites us to get personal.

In essence, Jesus says, "In me you have peace. In the world you have trouble. But take heart—I've overcome the world" (John 16:33). We live in specifics, not generalities. You are invited to come candidly with your particular afflictions.

James says that you will "meet trials of *various* kinds" (James 1:2). These are the exact places where the Lord will develop steadiness and depth in your faith. In affliction you discover how you lack wisdom. So you ask for wisdom. And God freely gives what you need.

Peter says that you are "grieved by *various* trials" (1 Pet. 1:6). But in Christ you have been given something imperishable. God promises to guard you by his power and to make your faith more genuine and true as you pass through fire.

Paul says that our Father and our Lord Jesus Christ comfort us in "*all* our afflictions" (2 Cor. 1:4). Your troubles nestle within that promise. God will comfort and strengthen you, giving you a growing ability to help others in whatever troubles they face.

David prays for himself,

> Turn to me and be gracious to me,
>> for I am lonely and afflicted.
> The troubles of my heart are enlarged;
>> bring me out of my distresses. (Ps. 25:16–17)

And then he prays for all God's children,

> Redeem Israel, O God,
>> out of all his troubles. (25:22)

You are invited to bring your need, your troubles, your afflictions, your loneliness into the heart of God's grace and deliverance.

All these voices speak out of experiences like yours—different in the specifics, but hard in the same ways. So bring your own story into what we discuss together.

What is the most significant suffering you experienced in the past?

_____

What is the hardest thing you are facing now?

_____

What are you afraid you might have to go through someday?

_____

Think about it and get specific. Write in the margins of these pages. Keep thinking when you put the book down. Pray about it. Talk it out with your best friend tomorrow. Walk it out. The title of this book is intentional. We are not going to discuss the general topic of God and suffering. We will consider how God's grace enters directly into *your* suffering.

Don't rush on. Pull out a pen or pencil. Take five or ten minutes—or more, if that's the honest thing to do.

Where are you struggling to make sense of things?

_____

Where do you need help?

_____

Where do you need wisdom?

_____

Where do you need courage?

_____

Where do you need mercy?

_____

Where do you need protection?

_____

Where do you need strength?

_____

The gifts of God's grace fit hand-in-glove with your need. *You* are responsible for half of this book! If you do your part well, it will be the better half.

Let me prime the pump a bit more to get you thinking broadly. Perhaps one catastrophic event leapt to mind. But as you think further, maybe something else presses forward into consciousness. Perhaps the searing moment has not been as significant as some difficult, disappointing relationship that has lasted a long, long time. There are many kinds of significant suffering. Sometimes something seemingly small is the perfect laboratory for growing in grace. Your Redeemer invites you to consider any life-troubling situation, whether large or small, and then to make it personal. None of us suffers in general. Each of us struggles in particular ways. You can put your particulars on the table.

Here is still another way to come at this. What has marked you? More specifically, what marked you for good? Profound good in our lives often emerges in a crucible of significant suffering. Jesus himself "learned obedience through what he suffered" (Heb. 5:8). Faith and love shine most clearly, simply, and courageously in a dark place.

And, what has marked you for bad? Our typical sins emerge in reaction to betrayal, loss, or pain. Hammered by some evil, we discover evils operating in our own hearts. We feel resentful, anxious, desperate, overwhelmed, confused—or all of the above!

Perhaps most often, both the bad and the good come out of us. A trial brings out what is most wrong, and God brings about what is most right as he meets you and works with you. So the psalm writer says,

> Before I was afflicted I went astray,
> but now I keep your word. (Ps. 119:67)

Affliction itself is not good, but God works what is very good, bringing the ignorant and wayward back home. Faith's enduring and alert dependency on the Lord is one of the Spirit's finest fruits. And you bear that fruit only when you have lived through something hard.

2

HOW FIRM A FOUNDATION

You have experienced, you are experiencing, and you will experience afflictions. I've asked you to refer to your experience, and in the pages that follow I will also refer to mine.

We have good role models for our candor! We see the afflictions of Abraham, Jacob, and Joseph. We see the children of Israel first enslaved and then wandering. We see Naomi and then Hannah. We see David and then Jeremiah. We see Jesus and then Paul. They talked openly of their afflictions, and they revealed God's ways as they grieved, prayed, spoke, taught, and worshiped from within honest experience.

The chapters that follow will weave together four strands of testimony. Of course Scripture, your experience, and my experience will appear. The fourth strand will be a wise hymn, "How Firm a Foundation." I've chosen this hymn because it expresses how an unknown brother or sister captures God's grace at work within suffering. Do read through this hymn carefully. Sing it if you're so moved. And read it again. Feel free to underline or to comment on what strikes you as a first impression.

How firm a foundation, you saints of the Lord,
is laid for your faith in his excellent Word!
What more can he say than to you he has said,
to you who for refuge to Jesus have fled?

"Fear not, I am with you, O be not dismayed;
for I am your God, and will still give you aid;
I'll strengthen you, help you, and cause you to stand,
upheld by my righteous, omnipotent hand.

"When through the deep waters I call you to go,
the rivers of sorrow shall not overflow;
for I will be with you, your troubles to bless,
and sanctify to you your deepest distress.

"When through fiery trials your pathway shall lie,
my grace, all-sufficient, shall be your supply;
the flame shall not hurt you; I only design
your dross to consume and your gold to refine.

"E'en down to old age all my people shall prove
my sovereign, eternal, unchangeable love;
and when hoary hairs shall their temples adorn,
like lambs they shall still in my bosom be borne.

"The soul that on Jesus has leaned for repose,
I will not, I will not desert to his foes;
that soul, though all hell should endeavor to shake,
I'll never, no never, no never forsake."[1]

24

In this chapter I will make two introductory comments about the whole hymn and will encourage you to probe other hymns that also speak to your suffering. Then in subsequent chapters we will explore the meaning and implications of each stanza.

The Author and the Voice

1. *Whose hymn is it?* One of the subtle charms of "How Firm a Foundation" is that it is anonymous. Only God and the author know who wrote it. In a world obsessed with taking credit and receiving payment for achievements, this hymn is simply an unknown person's honest offering to God. What significant sufferings had that person faced? We don't know. But every stanza breathes firsthand experience with God's hand in life's hardships. Was the author male or female? Young or old? Married or single? Black, brown, or white? Rich, poor, or middling? Baptist, Presbyterian, or Anglican? We don't know. Whoever the person was, whatever distresses made life tumultuous, we hear timely words from the Lord who personally intervenes. These words from your brother or sister will speak into *your* significant suffering. The anonymity adds appropriateness to the invitation to make this hymn your very own as a means of grace.

2. *Whose voice speaks through it?* We don't always pay attention to this, but every hymn adopts a point of view, a voice that identifies a speaker and a listener. For example, many hymns, like many psalms, sing directly *to God*. In singing "Be Thou my vision, O Lord of my heart!,"[2] you give voice to your need and express your love.

Other hymns, like other psalms, sing *about God to each other*. In the words "Amazing grace, how sweet the sound, that saved a wretch like me,"[3] you proclaim what our Lord has done for you. In "O come, all ye faithful,"[4] you call your brothers and sisters to wake up and adore our Lord.

Occasionally, as in Psalm 103, a hymn has you sing *to yourself*. In the lyric "Be still, my soul; the Lord is on your side,"[5] you proclaim hope to yourself when you are agitated and anxious. And in "Arise, my soul, arise, shake off your guilty fears,"[6] you proclaim hope to yourself when you feel crushed by your sins.

Whether spoken to God, to each other, or to ourselves, we give voice to our faith, our need, and our joy. But in "How Firm a Foundation," you sing in an unusual voice. Only in the first stanza do you talk about the Lord and call each other to listen to what he has said. In the rest of the hymn, *God is talking directly to you*. Notice that each of the last five stanzas begins with a quotation mark. These are the Lord's words. Though we sing these words, we are placed in the role of listeners—as in Psalm 50:5–23.

God is talking to you. Ponder that. You sing this hymn by listening intently. What does the Lord talk about? Interestingly, he is speaking directly into your significant suffering. He tells you who he is, and what he is like, and what he is doing—not in general, but with respect to what you are going through. He breathes his purposes into your heartaches. He promises the very things you most need. Most hymns express our faith—to God, to each other, or to ourselves. This hymn is more elemental. God's voice invites faith. He's calling to you.

This is particularly appropriate when it comes to suffering. The hymn writer demonstrates a profound feel for the struggles and needs of sufferers. A sufferer's primal need is to hear God talking and to experience him purposefully at work. When you hear, take to heart, and know that he is with you, everything changes, even when nothing has changed in your situation. Left to yourself, you blindly react. Your troubles obsess you, distract you, depress you. You grasp at straws. God seems invisible, silent, far away. Threat and pain and loss cry out long and loud. Faith seems inarticulate. Sorrow and confusion broadcast on all the channels. It's hard to remember anything else, hard to put into words what is actually happening, hard to feel any of the force of who Jesus Christ is.

You might mumble right answers to yourself, but it's like reading the phone book. You pray, but your words sound rote, vaguely unreal, mere pious generalities. You'd never talk to a real person that way. Meanwhile, the struggle churning within you is anything but rote and unreal. The pressure and hurt become completely engrossing. You're caught in a swirl of apprehension, anguish, regret, confusion, bitterness, emptiness, uncertainty.

This struggle is not surprising. Exodus 6:9, for example, describes how "despondency and cruel bondage" deafened the people (NASB). They felt so crushed that Moses's words made no impression. I suspect we've all felt that way sometimes. Words that someone else finds meaningful and thinks might be helpful are just words, empty sounds with no meaning.

But God works to reverse the downward spiral into deafness

and despair. As the story in Exodus unfolds, the Lord continues to say what he does and do what he says. The people's sufferings, deafness, and blindness did not vanish in the twinkling of an eye. But by Exodus 15, the people were seeing and hearing, and they sang with hearty, well-founded joy.

How much more do the Lord's voice and hand reach us in our times. The Holy Spirit works powerfully and intimately in this age of new creation to communicate God's words, presence, and love into our hearts. Sufferers awaken to hear their Father's voice and to see their Savior's hand in the midst of significant suffering.

You need to hear what God says, and to experience that he does what he says. You need to feel the weight and significance of what he is about. He never lies. He never disappoints (though he wisely sets about to disappoint our false hopes, that we might be freed of our illusions). Though you walk through the valley of the shadow of death, you need fear no evil. He is with you. Goodness and mercy will follow you. This *is* what he is doing. God's voice speaks deeper than what hurts, brighter than what is dark, more enduring than what is lost, truer than what has happened.

You awaken. You take it to heart, and you take heart. You experience that this is so. The world changes. You change. His voice changes the meaning of every hardship. What he does— has done, is doing, will do—alters the impact and outcome of everything happening to you. Your faith grows up into honest, intelligent humanness, no longer murky and inarticulate. You grow more like Jesus: the man of sorrows acquainted with grief, the man after God's own heart, who having loved his own, loved them to the end.

Making It Personal for You

As we unpack ways in which "How Firm a Foundation" communicates God's grace into the troubles we face, I encourage you to be gathering other resources of grace to strengthen and encourage you.

For example, what other hymns and songs have spoken to you, lifting your heart up from dark places into Christ? Here are two classic hymns that often encourage me when I am burdened.

1. *A hymn that you sing about the Lord—and can also sing to the Lord.* The title "Jesus! What a Friend for Sinners!"[7] communicates only half of the hymn's story. Jesus is also a true friend for sufferers. Wilbur Chapman is honest about life's hardships. He speaks about friends who let you down. He tells of people who are not friends at all but are out to hurt you. He knows what it is like to feel brokenhearted, sad, and weak. He has experienced stormy times and dark nights. By giving these examples and metaphors, Chapman invites you to make it personal. And, most of all, he reminds you in a dozen different ways that Jesus is right here when your life is hard. He hears your cry for help.

Throughout this hymn we sing *about* how the Lord connects to our struggles. But for many years our congregation has pointedly altered the last stanza and final refrain so that we sing these directly *to* our Savior:

Jesus, I do now receive *you*,
    more than all in *you* I find;
You have granted me forgiveness,
    I am *yours*, and *you* are mine.
Hallelujah! What a Savior!
    Hallelujah! What a Friend!
Saving, helping, keeping, loving,
    you are with me to the end.

I have found it personally very meaningful to shift to direct I-you language in the climax of the hymn. Hymns typically are written in a single voice, as is standard English. But Scripture models a more flexible way with words. It often shifts back and forth, like what our church has done with this hymn. For example, Psalm 23 begins and ends by talking about who the Lord is and what he does. But in the darkest valley, I speak directly: "*You* are with me."

2. *A hymn that you sing to yourself.* Katharina von Schlegel had experienced the death of her dearest friends. She felt grief, pain, tears, sorrow, fears, and disappointment. In "Be Still, My Soul," she wrestles within herself, seeking to find calm in the midst of agitation and upset. She reminds herself from many angles that her best Friend is with her. He will wipe away all her tears on the day he restores love's purest joys. Christ will do the same for you.

In addition to hymns, many fine books have been written on suffering. You will not go wrong with books by Nancy Guthrie and by Joni Eareckson Tada. A lesser-know book that is very thoughtful is Dan McCartney's *Why Does It Have to Hurt?*[8]

Like other vast and important topics—the gospel of Jesus Christ, the struggle with sin, what love looks like—there is room for a fresh angle. Because the wise and helpful books all drink from the same living stream, they complement each other. No two of them come at the topic from the same angle or say exactly the same thing. My hope is that this book, while not attempting to say everything, offers a few things that you will find helpful.

3

LISTEN WELL

Paul wrote, "The firm foundation of God stands, having this seal, 'The Lord knows those who are his'" (2 Tim. 2:19). This excellent Word never changes. The Lord knows you. This reality is the single most important thing about you. You are his. This truth makes the decisive difference in how you walk down hard roads. Our hymn begins by inviting us to build our lives on this reality.

> How firm a foundation, you saints of the Lord,
> is laid for your faith in his excellent Word!
> What more can he say than to you he has said,
> to you who for refuge to Jesus have fled?

Consider three things about the affirmation and rhetorical question in this opening stanza.

What More Can He Say?

First, the question: "What more can he say than to you he has said?" Let that rattle around a minute. I don't know how you read Scripture. But there is a way to read Scripture that leaves you wishing God had said a whole lot more. How did Satan become evil? Why does Chronicles add zeros to the numbers in Samuel and Kings? How did Jonah avoid asphyxiation? Who wrote the book of Hebrews? And those aren't even the questions that most often divide and perplex the church. Wouldn't it have been great if the Lord had slipped in one killer verse that pins down the timetable for the return of Christ? That resolves every question about the meaning and mode of baptism and the Lord's Supper? That specifically informs us how to organize church leadership and government? That tells us exactly what sort of music to use in worship? That explains how God's sovereign purposes dovetail with human responsibility? That describes just how the Holy Spirit intends and does not intend to express his dynamic power?

If we only had one more verse on each of the top ten questions we wrangle over! And think what he could have told us with an extra paragraph or chapter on a few of the tough topics! If only the Lord had shortened the genealogies, omitted a few villages in the land distribution, and condensed the spec sheet for the temple's dimensions, dishware, decor, and duties. Our Bible would be exactly the same length—even shorter—but the questions that rattle the church could have been anticipated and definitively answered. But somehow, God in his providence didn't choose to do that.

It comes down to what you are looking for as you read and listen. When you get to what most matters, to life-and-death issues, *what more can he say than to you he has said?* To whom do you entrust your life? What will happen to you? Are you facing betrayal by someone you trusted? Aggressive, incurable cancer? A disfiguring disability? Your most persistent sin? These are what Scripture is about. And God's words address all the defining existential questions—questions about meaning or despair in the face of death, purpose or pointlessness, good or evil, love or hate, trust or fear, truth or lies. Can mercy untangle the knot of sin? Can justice undo oppression? What about the character of God? The dynamics of the human heart? The meaning of affliction? What more can the Lord say than to you he has said? Listen well. There is nothing more that he needs to say.

You Saints

Second, consider the name by which this opening stanza describes you. You are one of the Lord's "saints." In a nutshell, God is saying, *"You are mine. You belong to me."* He knows his own. In popular usage, the word "saint" has been debased to describe extraordinary, individual spiritual achievements. But in the Bible—where *God* defines sainthood—the word describes ordinary people who belong to a most extraordinary Savior and Lord. Our Redeemer achieves all the extraordinary things. At our best (and too often we are at our worst, or bumping along in the middle!), "we have done only that which we ought to have done" (Luke 17:10 NASB). God calls you a saint to point out who owns you, not to honor you for going above and beyond the call of duty. It's not the Medal of Honor. It's your enlistment papers and dog tag. When God has written his name on you, suffering qualitatively changes. Pain, loss, and weakness are no longer the end of the world and the death of your hopes.

Because God calls you "his chosen ones, holy and beloved" (Col. 3:12), you will dwell in his house forever. This frees you to bend your life energies toward growing more childlike toward him and more helpful toward others. Your hopes will come true in ways far beyond your wildest dreams.

If you are not his saint, then losses and disappointments— yesterday's, today's, and tomorrow's—are omens of the end of all that you value, long for, and strive for. All that you live for will die when you die (Prov. 10:28). Your fears will come true. This is not just because of some far-off judgment day. This is simply the self-evident logic of your death. But come into the life and love of Christ. Then sufferings and losses become a context in which true hopes awaken and strengthen. You have been given an inheritance that is imperishable. Your hopes will come true. This is simply the self-evident logic of the reality that Jesus is alive. Christian faith does not make a leap of faith into the dark. Not believing makes the leap—a leap of unbelief into the dark, betting with your life that Jesus is not alive and well. To be a Christian is to walk on a path that is like the light of dawn, which shines brighter and brighter until full day.

For Refuge

Third, this stanza says something else very significant about you. You have taken refuge in the Lord. You are a "refugee." You fled for your life, and have found every sort of aid and protection in Jesus.

In September 2005, hundreds of thousands of people in Louisiana, Mississippi, and Alabama were displaced by Hurricane Katrina. Many escaped with nothing—and lost everything. They were vulnerable. They needed food, housing, medical care, clothes, money, police protection, a new start. But a public official caused an uproar when he referred to the evacuees as "refugees." The term was seen as demeaning. It called to mind the degraded conditions in refugee camps for those fleeing genocide in Bosnia or Sudan.

We, however, are glad refugees. The word might connote degradation to some, but in Christ it becomes an affirmation of glory and hope. We *are* refugees, migrants, homeless people, displaced persons, distressed travelers, aliens, and wanderers looking for our true homeland. The Bible turns so many typical associations upside down. Words for powerlessness and shame—*slave, needy, crucified, weak, refugee*—invert into symbols of joy. People fleeing disaster have no safe place, are vulnerable, and depend absolutely on outside mercies. But you have found all you need and more than you could ever imagine in the Lord, the only true refuge.

The opposite of being a refugee? You hear that message everywhere: Believe in yourself. Be self-confident, self-sufficient, and self-assertive. Be independent. Affirm yourself. You are entitled, so boldly assert your opinions, and say whatever you think and feel. You are free to do and be just what you want. This is our culture's dream, and it is delusional. Point by point, it exactly describes the kind of person that Proverbs calls a fool. To live as a fool is disastrous.

But to live as a refuge seeker is to live. Life as a refugee, a migrant, is often unpleasant. Does it feel good to "trust in the LORD with all your heart" (Prov. 3:5)? Does dependency mean feeling safe, warm, secure, and comfortable? Sometimes. A child on his mother's lap rests in peaceful trust, as Psalm 131 captures it. But even that psalm describes a peace that comes only after wrestling within yourself. In most psalms, faith means trusting someone else in a dicey, dangerous situation.

It is unsettling to *need* help. Even when it ends up joyous and peaceful, dependency often doesn't feel very good in the process. You must cast your cares on God, who cares for you, because you're helpless in yourself (1 Pet. 5:7). Your cares are bigger than you. You are under pressure. You are vulnerable, and you know it. You are burdened about matters you cannot control or fix. Life is hard. You feel crushed, careworn, threatened. You come as a refugee, not boasting of your assets, but bringing your cares. And your Father cares for you. He is strong and good. Safe at last! In the end, you rest peacefully.

Psalm 28 captures the whole cycle in a short space. David basically cries out, "Help. If you won't listen to me, I will die." That is not a comfortable feeling. He is threatened, battered, and exposed. He is powerless, with nowhere else to turn. The Lord does listen. The outcome is exultant and grateful.

> He has heard the voice of my pleas for mercy.
> The LORD is my strength and my shield;
> in him my heart trusts, and I am helped;
> my heart exults,
> and with my song I give thanks to him. (28:6–7)

38

The voice of need becomes a voice of joy: "You are so good!" The cry for help becomes a shout of gratitude: "Thank you!" It's not pleasant to *need* help. But it's sheer joy to *find* help.

When Jesus says that "the poor in spirit" are the blessed (Matt. 5:3), he turns another pejorative word upside down. "Poor" describes refugees and other beggars. "Poor in spirit" means you are fully aware of the reality that you are destitute. You are conscious of dire and pressing need for help that God must give. And God most freely and generously gives, blessing you with nothing less than his presence in the kingdom of life! Insoluble suffering (like insoluble sin) brings you in through the door of all blessing. God does not turn away from the afflictions of the afflicted. So do not be afraid, little flock—he is giving you the kingdom.

Our discipleship materials don't often teach us much about this. We learn how to have a quiet time. We discover our spiritual gifts. We study good doctrine. We learn how to study the Bible and memorize Scripture. These are all good things. But we don't necessarily learn how to need help. "How Firm a Foundation" teaches you to need help. God uses significant suffering to teach us to need him. And when we need him, we find him.

My Story

This book is born of experience, not proposed as a theory. At several points in this book I will tell a bit of my own story.

A number of years ago I flew out to the Midwest from Philadelphia to meet with two groups who were trying to resolve their differences. Six of us sat around the table talking through issues that had frayed relationships. The outcome was fruitful for the parties involved. But during that long day of candid, constructive discussion, something very unusual and disturbing kept happening to me. On at least a half dozen occasions I would begin to say something, and halfway through I would completely lose my train of thought. Over and over again, whatever point I was trying to make fizzled out. I had no idea what I was trying to say. It was unnerving.

I flew home late, and as I lay in bed that night, I reflected on what had happened. It was distressing. My work involves teaching, counseling, and writing. You might say that it's my job to complete my thoughts! If I can't remember what I'm trying to say, then I can't do what I'm supposed to do. Like a pitcher in baseball who experiences a career-ending injury, I faced the distressing possibility of life-altering loss.

In the silence and darkness, I prayed my troubles to God. My prayers were basic: "Lord, you say you are a very present help in trouble. . . . This is trouble. . . . Help." And it was mildly encouraging that in reconstructing what had happened that day, I could piece together what I had intended to say. But two other considerations proved far more helpful.

The first consideration was something my pastor had instilled twenty-five years earlier. He actively discipled the small group leaders and seminary students in our congregation. He would get pointedly personal in alerting us to the danger of turning *gifts* into an identity and *ministry* into an idolatry. He challenged us to do a thought experiment: "What if you were in a car accident and had a permanent brain injury? You were no longer able to do the things you now love doing. Could you be content working at MacDonald's, restocking supplies, emptying trash, mopping floors, and cleaning bathrooms?"

We needed to able to answer, "Yes, I would do such work willingly." We might grieve our injury and loss, certainly. But, in the end, it was supremely important that we could be content doing any honorable work. And keeping a restaurant clean is honorable. Janitorial work does active good to patrons, fellow workers, and employers.

Part of my pastor's point was that, by design, your gifts are just that—on loan from God for a useful purpose. And, by design, ministry is menial work. It means being a servant, someone's assistant, a helper. You are running errands. You lay down your life so that another person's life might go better. Discontentment and complaining reveal pride, as if menial work were "beneath me."

Over the years I'd often done this thought experiment as a check on my attitude. That night, as I lay there in silence and darkness, it wasn't theoretical. I had repeatedly been unable to do what my current job required. Would it be okay if a temporary gift were now no longer mine to use? Can I be fundamentally content?

The second consideration came from 2 Corinthians 12. This Scripture runs in the same path as the thought experiment. Paul describes how the Lord allowed him to be afflicted with persistent weakness and pain in order to guard him from pride. He had pleaded for the Lord to take away what was so distressing. But God replied, "My grace is sufficient for you, for my power is made perfect in weakness" (12:9). The core principle of the gospel is that Christ's grace and strength are demonstrated in our need. Paul got that point. He was content amid all sorts of troubles and limitations. He was living out the core principle of Christian faith: "When I am weak, then I am strong" (12:10).

That night I wrestled these things through. "Is this really true? Is Christ true, right now, after I've had such an unsettling day, facing such a threat?" I turned it over in my heart, pondering and praying. By the Lord's grace and power, I came to a peaceful conclusion. When he says, "My grace is sufficient for you," it's true. I didn't like what was happening, but the bottom line: I could say, "It's okay. I am not living for my abilities. If I am to be disabled, then deep, deep down, that's okay."

My heart grew quiet. I relaxed and started to drift toward sleep. But then one more thing came to mind. Coming to terms with a profound personal and spiritual issue cleared mental space to consider what I should do practically. I happened to remember that I had started to take a new cholesterol medication a few days earlier. The doctor hadn't said anything about side effects. But I should call the doctor or the pharmacist in the morning. It was a small step: "Call tomorrow for some information." What I was facing was huge: "I could be losing the ability to do the work I've been doing for the past twenty-five years, the work that I love, the work that supports my family." But as with most of life, our concerns are bigger than our ability. I slept.

In the morning, I left a message with my doctor's office but reached the pharmacist in person. I described what had happened. She replied, "Is this what it's like? You get in your car to drive to the 7-Eleven a mile away. You get three blocks from home and completely forget where you're going. You get lost on the way." I said, "You are describing it exactly—getting lost on the way." She said, "That mental disruption is a known side effect of this medication. Stop taking it." I stopped, and the problem did not recur.

May God be praised! That was a significant day. I am very grateful that I did not become mentally disabled at that time, that this particular suffering proved amenable to a cure. But I am even more grateful—profoundly grateful—for how Christ met me and proved true in a time of need. It is eternally significant that the thought experiment proved true when it became a matter of reality, not theory. I love the ministry of putting words into sentences that I hope will help someone. But it is guaranteed that someday I will no longer be able to do this thing I love. And it is so important that the ability to complete a thought does not define who I am. I am weak; Christ is strong. I am a refugee fleeing into his care. I am one of his own.

Making It Personal for You

When he engages your suffering, the all-wise God typically creates a dynamic interplay of five questions:

1. What hardship are you facing?
2. What life-giving word from God speaks to you?
3. What input do wise friends give you?
4. How can you honestly wrestle your way toward trusting God?
5. What should you do next?

You saw God at work in each of these elements in the story I just told. Walk this through for yourself.

1. *What hardship are you facing?* The first question is easy to answer, because life lands on your head with something hard. What are you facing? If you've chosen a crushing, multidimensional affliction, perhaps start with one small slice of the far larger problem. God's ways with us always respect that we can only take the next step. No leaping tall buildings at a single bound.

2. *What life-giving word from God speaks to you?* The second question has many possible answers. Do you already have in mind something true from and about our God that speaks relevantly to you in your situation? When I experienced losing my way mentally, 2 Corinthians 12 put together the Lord's power and my weakness. Those words "wear the clothes" of what I was experiencing. What has been helpful to you in the past? Or do you need something fresh about who the Lord is? Read in parts of Scripture where suffering provides the backdrop. Psalms, Job, 2 Corinthians, and 1 Peter are the usual suspects. But many other parts of Scripture touch on our afflictions. Is there a song that reminds you of who you are in God's sight? A psalm that honestly relates to him in the middle of a struggle? A teaching point from a sermon or book that speaks to how God works in affliction? A promise of what the Lord will do in the future?

3. *What input do wise friends give you?* The third question is very important but can be complicated to answer. You need other people. It's easy to forget this and try to fly solo through hard times. Who can walk with you? Ask yourself: "Who is the

person I most trust? Who will handle with care the fine china of my honest struggles? Who will draw me out and listen well. Who keeps confidences, prays thoughtfully, and is willing to speak candidly with godly wisdom? Who is the most sensible, straightforward, humble, believing, experienced, courageous person I know?" None of your friends is perfect! But God puts imperfect people in our lives who are also wise, caring, and trustworthy—the kind of person you want to be for others. Who can share the burden with you, will cast your cares on God, will encourage you?

Part of the complexity of question 3 comes because other people can be foolish—even very foolish. They can be like Job's counselors and treat you wrong. They might offer bad counsel. They might make foolish promises that aren't at all true about God and how he works within tough situations. They might be meddlesome and just try to fix you. They might be untrustworthy and prone to gossip. So you can't ask just anyone to walk with you.

My pastor was the significant person in the small story I told, even though he had passed away some years earlier. My wife was asleep. But the way my pastor had tutored my faith still spoke to me that dark night.

4. *How can you honestly wrestle your way toward trusting God?* The fourth question gets you wrestling to make what is true your own. Strive to remember and take to heart truth that is easy to forget. Seek the Lord honestly. In turning toward him, you will likely be turning away from instinctive and habitual sins. Anxiety? Anger? Despair? Escapism? He is merciful. He

"opposes the proud but gives grace to the humble" (James 4:6). Don't be afraid to tell the Lord the truth about your sufferings, your sins, your desires for mercy, your struggles. Dozens of psalms have walked that road. Ask your Father to give you his Holy Spirit. All wisdom, trust, peace, courage, love, endurance, and hope are the fruit of his personal touch.

Honest wrestling is not magic. It's not "claiming the victory." It's not finding a religious truism to short-circuit the process. And it's not wallowing in heartache and self-pity. God is taking us in his direction. Ask. Seek. Knock. He found you first, and he is willing to be found.

5. *What should you do next?* The fifth question gets you thinking about the practical "What now?" In significant suffering, the problem is always much bigger than what you are called to do now, but that doesn't preclude taking meaningful steps. I couldn't fix the distressing things that had happened that day, but I could make a couple of phone calls. Katharina von Schlegel couldn't bring back her beloved friends, but she could put her soul's struggle into a poem that we still sing, "Be Still, My Soul." What is a small but significant next step for you? It may be as simple as getting up from prayer and calling a friend, or doing the laundry, or paying your bills, or going to work, or taking a personal day to walk in the park.

4

I AM WITH YOU

In the setting of the entire hymn "How Firm a Foundation," stanzas 2–6 appear within quotation marks (I will not repeat the marks with the individual stanzas). *You* read and sing the words, but *your God himself* is talking with you:

Fear not, I am with you, O be not dismayed;
for I am your God, and will still give you aid;
I'll strengthen you, help you, and cause you to stand,
upheld by my righteous, omnipotent hand.

I will focus on two things he is saying, and then I will unpack one very important implication.

Reactions to Avoid

Notice how this stanza describes our inward experience of hardship. How do you react to serious suffering? "Fear" and "dismay" cover the ground pretty well! If you are honest, you feel rocked, overwhelmed, preoccupied, confused, upset, endangered. You struggle—always. Struggle describes a wrestling match going on inside. You are grappling with something. If you did not feel the pressure or the knife-edge of what is happening to you, you'd be a stone, not a human being. God's image bearers are not impervious.

Up to a point, fear and dismay are natural reactions. But problems arise when distress and apprehension become Godless. The honest anguish of faith slips into godless upset. As troubles settle in, they claim your thought life, conversations, emotions, future, faith. They occupy wakeful hours at night. If you fall asleep, they wake up with you first thing in the morning. Dismay well covers a whole range of temptations—tendencies from troubled to unglued, from disappointed to hopeless, from worried to panicky, from frustrated to enraged.

There are also the dishonest reactions that aim to silence dismay in the face of life's troubles. Some people intentionally mute dismaying realities by doing mental gymnastics that keep suffering at arm's length. But Scripture never commends stoics. Other people become cynical, hard-boiled, brutal, and invulnerable—not likely readers of a book with "Your Suffering" in the title! But Scripture never commends cynics. Other people recoil from life, so fearful of being hurt that they withdraw into a shell of excruciating self-protection. Wishing to avoid pain is natural, but Scripture never commends isolation as a strategy. Some people escape pain into the false, feel-good refuges of entertainment, recreation, food, drink, and drugs. But Scripture never commends addiction as a way to handle pain.

Scripture does commend honestly facing weakness and pain—as Jesus and the Psalms did—both for integrity's sake and in order to love others who also suffer. Honesty feels the weight of things that arouse fear and dismay—because fearsome and dismaying things do happen to us. Hardships give us good reasons to be anxious, so God gives better reasons to trust him. The problem is not that we feel troubled by trouble and pained by pain. Something hurtful should hurt. The problem is that God slides away into irrelevance when we obsess over suffering or compulsively avoid it. God inhabits a vague afterthought—weightless and distant in comparison to the thing immediately pressing upon us. Or we fabricate a god who will magically make everything better if we can only catch his ear. Pain naturally triggers a cascade of apprehension, unhappiness, and distress and, because of the deviance of our hearts, often triggers bad reactions of unbelief and idolatry. That is, unless we remember what our hymn's second stanza is telling us.

Promises to Embrace

Notice what else God says. Though we have good reasons for apprehension, he gives a cascade of better reasons that invite the finest responses of which a human being is capable. These reasons patterned Jesus's consciousness, motives, emotions, words, and actions as he faced his own significant suffering.

In our second stanza, God makes seven promises that speak to our fear and dismay. The hymn writer didn't just make them up. The stanza closely paraphrases Isaiah 41:10. God spoke these words, and the hymn accurately quotes and then slightly amplifies them so that the lyrics sustain a singable rhyme and rhythm. I've put the Lord's exact words in italics and the amplifications in brackets:

> *Fear not, for I am with you;*
>> *be not dismayed, for I am your God;*
>> [and I will still give you aid.]
> *I will strengthen you, I will help you,*
>> [and I will cause you to stand.]
>> *I will uphold you with my righteous* [omnipotent] *right hand.*

Jesus, the pioneer and perfecter of faith, heard this voice and took it to heart. He now says these same things to you.

Are you listening?

We may have a hard time slowing down enough to listen. We might simply not want to listen. We may be busy listening to ten thousand other voices, including our own. Or we may feel so weary and disheartened that we don't feel up to listening. But whatever the particulars, our essential problem is deafness to God's voice. We become absorbed in the world of our own experiences, thoughts, feelings, and opinions.

A striking Latin phrase captures the essential inward-turning nature of sinfulness: *incurvatus in se*. We curve in on ourselves. Sin's *incurvatus in se* pointedly turns away from God. When you (or others) suffer, you experience (or witness) the strength of this incurving tendency. It's hard not to be self-preoccupied.

But God willingly keeps talking. Listen to how near he

sounds in this hymn. The Lifegiver gives us ears to hear. The incurving can be reversed. Scripture itself models this. Psalms cry out, rather than turning in. Jesus is a most excellent teacher. In the extremity of his agony, there was no *incurvatus in se*. He heard God's voice and remembered. He turned toward God in neediness, generosity, and trust: "My God, my God, why have you forsaken me?" "Forgive them, for they know not what they do." "Father, into your hands I commit my spirit!" (Matt. 27:46; Luke 23:34, 46). He turned toward people in practical love: "Today you will be with me in paradise." "Behold, your son! . . . Behold, your mother!" (Luke 23:43; John 19:26–27). He gave voice to honest experience of his ordeal: "I thirst. . . . It is finished" (John 19:28, 30).

This is the Jesus to whom we have fled for refuge. This most careful and thoughtful of listeners walked ahead of us. He now deals gently with our ignorance and waywardness as he walks with us, fully aware of our temptations to be forgetful, distracted, and inattentive. He addresses the biggest problem first. That's why this hymn speaks in the first person. The words of new life first create ears that listen.

God is talking. His sheep hear his voice, even in the valley of the shadow of death. Are you listening?

The starting point of this stanza is well chosen: "I am with you." It is the central promise in all of Scripture, and the central promise we communicate in speaking pastorally with sufferers. Why can David say, "I will fear no evil" when he faces danger and the threat of death? "For you are with me," he continues (Ps. 23:4). You are not alone, not abandoned, not ignored, no matter what is happening. It is no accident that this is the central promise of the entire Bible, the one hope of sinners and sufferers. It is the only thing Moses really wanted, and without which the so-called Promised Land was only mediocre real estate. It is the essential reason that David's life flourished. And it came to a point in Immanuel. When God comes in person to walk with us, all his promises become "Yes" and "Amen" (2 Cor. 1:19–20).

"I am with you" is also a reality that we embody with each other. Though the presence of a brother or sister in Christ does not replace God, the nearness of another believer is a very significant means of God's grace. Christ's grace is embodied—in us, in each other. Other people are part of the comfort God brings to us in affliction.

The Problem with "the Problem"

Let me unpack one pastoral implication of the omni-relevant promise "I am with you."

Suffering often brings a doubled pain. In the first place there is "the problem" itself—perhaps sickness or poverty, betrayal or bereavement. That is hard enough. But it is often compounded by a second problem. Other people, even well-meaning, often respond poorly to sufferers. Sufferers are often misunderstood, or meddled with, or ignored. These reactions add relational and psychological isolation to the original problem.

For example, Job suffered the deaths of his children, financial disaster, and unrelenting physical pain. But then he had to deal with the attitudes of his wife and friends. They exacerbated his suffering. He became utterly isolated as they misunderstood and mistreated him. When Job's life was hardest, he was also most alone.

Similarly, Jesus faced betrayal, mockery, and torture at the hands of his enemies. As for his truest friends, first they argued about who was most important. Then they lapsed into sleepy incomprehension. Then they disintegrated into confusion, panic, flight, and denial. When Jesus's life was most painful, he also had to go it alone.

Doubled hardship is a common experience. A young woman is bereaved of her father, whom she dearly loves. Her friends are initially very supportive, but they get tired of her grief long before her grief is over. They give up on her as a friend. Or parents of a severely disabled child face lifelong hardships of many sorts. They also face how they are treated by others. Friends and family distance themselves, or feel awkward and don't know what to say, or offer woefully inappropriate help, or don't want to be bothered, or offer a thousand suggestions and fixes that reveal utter incomprehension of the realities. Disability is compounded by isolation.

Here's another way this happens. People who love you often focus exclusively on "the problem"—the hardship you are facing. They ask about the problem. They pray that God would solve the problem. They offer advice for solving the problem. Though they care for you and make well-meaning attempts to help, the effect can become quite unkind. They are missing *you*—the person facing the problem.

Many significant hardships have no remedy until the day

when all tears are wiped away: Your disease or disability is incurable. The injustice will not be remedied in your lifetime. Your loved one is dead. The marriage is over. The money is gone. There may be partial helps along the way, partial redemptions, but no fix.

But whether or not a problem is fixable, *you* are facing spiritual challenges. How are *you* doing? What are you learning? Where are you failing? Where do you need encouragement? Will you learn to live well and wisely within pain, limitation, weakness, and loss? Will suffering define you? Will faith and love grow, or will you shrivel up? These are life-and-death issues—more important than "the problem" in the final analysis. They take asking, thinking, listening, responding. They take time. Other people are often clumsy and incomprehending about the most important things, while pouring energy and love into solving what is often insoluble.

This double suffering commonly occurs when a health problem eludes diagnosis and cure. Jesus met "a woman who had had a discharge of blood for twelve years, and who had suffered much under many physicians, and had spent all that she had, and was no better but rather grew worse" (Mark 5:25–26). Her story has a decidedly contemporary ring! Bleeding was a real medical problem. But attempts to help multiplied her misery. The subsequent two thousand years have not eliminated the phenomenon: faulty diagnoses, misguided treatments, negative side effects, contradictory advice, huge wastes of time and money, false hopes repeatedly dashed, false fears pointlessly rehearsed, no plausible explanation forthcoming, blaming the victim, and declining sympathy as compassion fatigue sets in for would-be helpers! The woman was sick; other people made it worse.

J. I. Packer once noted that "a half-truth masquerading as the whole truth becomes a complete untruth."[1] We can extend his logic. A half-kindness masquerading as the whole kindness becomes a complete unkindness. The desire to explain and solve "the problem" is surely a kindness. But it can miss the person who must in any case come to grips with what is happening.

So whether you are abandoned because of your suffering or overshadowed by others' preoccupation with "the problem," the first line of our stanza displays a remarkable pastoral intuition. God speaks first to the fear, dismay, and isolation that attend our hardships. And he answers them with the monumental promise of his grace, "I am with you." He answers with himself.

My Story

My second story also arose in a medical situation. I had come down with diverticulitis multiple times over the previous year. My doctor, a woman who does not mince words, said, "You could die from one of these events. You need to get surgery—soon." So I did.

I awakened from anesthesia in the usual postoperative haze of stupor, pain, and thirst, along with the exceedingly slow march of time. That much was predictable. But something far more unsettling was also occurring. Everything seemed to be happening at a distance. I felt depersonalized. Life had a sense of unreality, emotional disconnect, internal disorientation. It was a dissociation experience. "I" had become detached from "myself," disconnected from the sense of myself as an experiencing, choosing, thinking person. It was as if I had been cut off from all the realities to which we are normally connected. You do not want this to happen to you. Not being able to complete one's thoughts is a mild concern compared with feeling disconnected from the very sense of being a person.

How do other people usually respond to someone in this state? Because it has a physiological substrate as a possible side-effect of anesthesia, the easiest response is to say, "Don't worry, it'll go away as your body reestablishes normal functioning." That was what the nurse told me. She viewed me as a malfunctioning body. True as far as it goes, but inside that body is a person experiencing something extremely distressing.

I phoned a trusted friend and sketched what was going on. To this day he has not been able to explain exactly why he did what he did next. He did not give me physiological information. He did not say, "Don't worry." He did not ask me questions. He did not try to counsel me. He did not pray for me. Instead he read the Psalms of Ascent, one after another, fifteen straight psalms without pause, without comment, from Psalm 120 through Psalm 134. He cared about me as a person immersed in a very unpleasant experience. He said later that the only thing he was thinking was that he knew I loved the Psalms. He figured reading psalms was a good thing because they are lucid, honest, sane, and full of the Lord. He was right.

When he finished, I was reconnected to myself. And then he prayed for me. And I gave heartfelt thanks to God. Psalms bring God and a person together.

Why and how did I change? I was changed because God found me when I could not even find myself. I was changed because words of faith are words of sanity and reality. I was changed because a friend did something unheard of. I was changed because a brutal side effect of anesthesia and major surgery made me need help. I was changed because I believed and knew and needed and trusted the Lord who is everywhere present in the Psalms—so I could hear his voice.

Making It Personal for You

Long ago, at many times and in many ways, God spoke to our fathers saying, "Don't be afraid." Our hymn captures the Lord's logic in Isaiah 41:10 as he responds to his people's struggle with hardship:

> RESPONSE: "Fear not."
> REASON: "For I am with you."
> RESPONSE: "Be not dismayed."
> REASON: "For I am your God."

Here's an earlier version of the same message, from Deuteronomy 31:8:

> REASON: "It is the LORD who goes before you. He will be with you; he will not leave you or forsake you."
> RESPONSE: "Do not fear or be dismayed."

And here's a subsequent version of that message, from Philippians 4:5–6:

REASON: "The Lord is near" (NIV).
RESPONSE: "Do not be anxious about anything."

Will you take that reason-and-response dynamic to heart? If you do, your life will never be the same. As you wrestle to take it to heart, the Lord will be rewriting the script of how you experience stress, anxiety, pressure, and threat.

Consider this chapter a workshop of sorts. Take your most significant suffering or some other hardship that tends to rattle and distress you, and fill in the blanks in these sentences:

Because it is true that _____,
    I am not afraid of _____.

I am not dismayed by _____,
    because _____.

Can you say this and mean it? What gets in the way? Wrestle it out with God, asking that he would write what is true on your heart.

To pray means to ask for something you need. A prayer is a request for help. Here's how I paraphrase Psalm 102:1–2 to bring out the intensity and honesty with which you can wrestle.

LORD, hear what I am asking.
Let my cry for help get through to you.
Don't hide your face from me in a time I find very
    distressing!

Lean in close, and really hear me.
At the very time I'm calling, quickly answer me!

You can talk that way with God. You need grace from the One who will save you. Right now. He gives you the reasons you can say it, mean it, and live it out all your days!

5

I AM WITH YOU
FOR A PURPOSE

The third stanza of "How Firm a Foundation" probes one of the deepest mysteries of how God meets us in our suffering:

> When through the deep waters I call you to go,
> the rivers of sorrow shall not overflow;
> for I will be with you, your troubles to bless,
> and sanctify to you your deepest distress.

Words from Isaiah 43 (especially 43:2) flow through this stanza. Our troubles are envisioned as deep waters and flooding rivers. Isaiah alludes to when God's people faced the Red Sea with enemies at their back, and to when they faced the Jordan River at flood stage. No human being could carve a path through such difficulties.

God again states his core promise, this time with an eye to

the future: "I will be with you." That itself is significant, because the effects of significant sufferings usually extend into an indeterminate future. We need much more than help in the present moment. What exactly does it mean that God will be with you amid destructive forces? What does it mean that he will "bless and sanctify" you amid your troubles and distress?

In promising this, God explicitly does *not* mean that he will give you mere comfort, warm feelings because a friend is standing at your side through tough times. God is at your side, but he plays a much more active and powerful role.

The Sovereign God's Care for His Own

This stanza fills in the meaning with four vast truths, four ways God personalizes on the "small screen" what he is doing on the "large screen" of Israel's history (the original context of Isaiah 43):

- God himself calls you into the deep waters.
- God sets a limit on your sorrows.
- God is with you, actively bringing good from your troubles.
- In the context of distressing events, God changes you.

This is heady stuff: high and purposeful sovereignty—a big God who comes close to speak tenderly, work personally, make you different, finish what he begins.

In other words, your significant sufferings don't happen by accident. There's no random chance. No purposeless misery. No bad luck. Not even (and understand this the right way) a tragedy. *Tragedy* means ruin, destruction, downfall, an unhappy ending with no redemption. Your life story may contain a great deal of misery and heartache along the way. But in the end, in Christ, your life story will prove to be a *comedy* in the original sense of the word, a story with a happy ending. You play a part in the *Divine Comedy*, as Dante called it, with the happiest ending of any story ever written. Death, mourning, tears, and pain will be no more (Rev. 21:4). Life, joy, and love get last say. High sovereignty is going somewhere.

People miss that when they make "the sovereignty of God" sound fatalistic and deterministic. But God's active providence in our affairs is not like Islamic *kismet*; or *que será será*; or just being realistic, philosophical, and resigned to life's hardships. God's sovereign purposes don't include the goal of just accepting your troubles. He's not interested in offering you some cognitive perspective to help get you through a rough patch. He is working so you know him, so you trust him, so you love him.

This stanza expresses the kind purposes of the Most High God. But it does not make light of your hardships. There is no chilly objectivity in these words. Every line carefully refers to the pain of deep sufferings. God speaks poignantly, not matter-of-factly, about "deep waters," "rivers of sorrow," "troubles," "deepest distress." In fact, the original hymn (with the eighteenth-century's *thee*s and *thou*s) expresses the second line even more graphically: "The rivers of woe shall not thee overflow." Woe is the keenest edge of anguish, the extremity of distress, sorrow raised to the highest degree of pain.

The rivers of woe shall not thee overflow.

Those rivers sweep many good things away. Your deepest

distress is deeply distressing. But the God who loves you is Master of your significant sorrow. He calls you to go through even this hard thing. Though woe feels impossible, though woe devastates earthly hopes, God sets a boundary (but not where we would set it). He convinces you that this hard thing will come to good beyond all you can ask, imagine, see, hear, or conceive in your heart (Eph. 3:20; 1 Cor. 2:9). You will pass through the valley of the shadow of death that is filled with evils and enemies. But you will come out saying that goodness and mercy followed you all the days of your life as you were coming home to your Shepherd's house (Psalm 23).

God is God. His reign is high and purposeful, yet reaches down into the details. But we often misapply God's sovereignty when it comes to actually helping sufferers—both ourselves and others. One common misapplication is to say, "God is in control, therefore what's happening is his will. You need to just trust the Lord and accept it. Ignore your feelings. Remember the truth. Gird your loins. Get with the program." Stoic conclusions are fashioned from a most unstoic truth about a most unstoic God! In the Bible, God is fiercely committed to his children's good. Part of that good is learning to be honest the way the Psalms are honest.

The Soul's Trust in the Sovereign's Care

The classic text whose pastoral application too often misfires into stoicism is 1 Peter 4:19: "Let those who suffer according to God's will entrust their souls to a faithful Creator while doing good." Even as you read those words, does it sound like the Bible puts the damper on heartache? Is Peter teaching a sanctified version of calm detachment and dutiful self-discipline? Is he saying: "It doesn't really matter that you're suffering. God's in control, so just keep up your quiet time and fulfill your responsibilities"? Does God make the deep waters only waist deep? Does he canalize the rivers of woe, so they flow gently between banks of riprap? Does he sanctify distress by making it unstressful? Does he call you to ignore what's going on around you in order to get on with being a Christian? Look carefully at *how* to entrust your soul to a faithful Creator. You'll never read 1 Peter 4:19 in the same way. What does that entrusting really look like?

First, consider David's Psalm 28 (paraphrased here). It gives a pithy, passionate example of what it means to entrust your soul to the sovereign God:

> To you, LORD, I call.
> My Rock, don't be deaf to me.
> If you don't answer me, I will die.
> Hear the voice of my supplications,
> my cry for help to you. (28:1–2)

These words are not calm, cool, and collected. David does not mentally rehearse the fact that God is in control in order to quietly press on with unflinching composure. Instead, he pleads candidly and believingly with God. He essentially cries out: "This is big trouble. You must help me. I need you. You are my only hope." Prayer means asking for something you need and want. Supplication means *really* asking. Frank supplication is the furthest thing from keeping everything in perspective so you can press on with life as normal. Supplication is not a calming exercise, like deep breathing. Supplication pleads for help from Someone who can help.

The sovereign God does not intend that you maintain the *status quo* while suffering. Pain disrupts normal. It's *supposed to* disrupt normal. It's supposed to make you feel a need for help. Psalm 28 is not a placid "quiet time." It's noisy and needy. When you let life's troubles get to you, it gets you to the only One who can help. As Psalm 28 unfolds, David specifically names the trouble he's in, what he's afraid of, what he wants. His trust in God's sovereign care moves to glad confidence. Finally, his faith works out into love. He starts interceding on behalf of others who also need to be strengthened, saved, protected, blessed, guided, and carried!

Second, consider how Psalm 10 expresses trust in a faithful God. Your life is being threatened by predatory people who give you good reason for apprehension. You begin to entrust your soul by crying out: "Why do you stand far away from me, O Lord? Where are you? Why do you hide yourself in times of trouble?" That is a plea of faith, not a bitter rant. It's the opposite of railing at God: "Where were you when I needed you? It's your fault that I'm suffering, because you could have stopped it." Both stoics and ranters take a mechanical view of God's sovereign control, detaching it from his loving purposes. For stoics, God's control over suffering rationalizes cool detachment. For ranters, it justifies hot accusation.

When you trust in God's sovereign rule, promises, and purposes, you talk out the implications with him. Instead of ignoring the situation and the feelings of threat, instead of finding a quiet (but unreal) solace, instead of just keeping busy by pressing on with business as usual, instead of ranting, the psalmist even takes time to think carefully about the thought processes of wicked men (10:2–11, 13). His scope of concern reaches beyond his own plight, to all those who are afflicted, unfortunate, innocent, orphaned, oppressed. He thinks through how God's hand rests differently on evildoers and on sufferers (10:12, 14–18). We might say that the things of earth definitely do *not* grow strangely dim. Instead, they grow much clearer in the light of his glory and grace! This psalm brings us to a place of resolution and confidence. But trust never anesthetizes the threat. So entrusting to a faithful Creator ends with a plea:

> Do justice to the fatherless and the oppressed,
>> so that man who is of the earth may strike terror no
>> more. (10:18)

That's not calm, cool, and collected. It's faith working through love.

Finally, Psalms 22:1 and 31:5 were on Jesus's lips because these psalms were in his heart as, on the cross, he entrusted his soul to God. Hebrews 5:7 refers back to this time as characterized by "loud cries and tears, to him who was able to save him from death." Jesus hardly ignored his feelings or viewed them as the inconvenient by-products of cognitive processes! The psalms he quoted gave voice to intense affliction. You see what was on Jesus's mind when he poured out his heart. He cried, "My God, my God, why have you forsaken me?" (Matt. 27:46; Mark 15:34) because he believed that the sovereign God does not treat lightly "the affliction of the afflicted"; that God won't shrink back in dismay from our troubles; that God doesn't turn away and ignore naked need (Ps. 22:24). He does not forsake us. He hears and acts. Other people often do distance themselves from suffering. They minimize it, recoil in distaste, look the other way, or blame the victim. But this God will hear our cry.

Jesus's final act of trust is expressed in words from Psalm 31:5: "Into your hands I commit my spirit!" (Luke 23:46). Taken out of context, those words might sound calm, cool, and collected. But taken in context, they are anything but calm. This is a plea of need from a man fully engaged with both his troubles and his God. The emotions of Psalm 31 express how faith trusts in the midst of danger and anguish. The emotions of faith run the gamut from fear to courage, from sorrow to joy, from hate to love, from neediness to gratitude.

Now, let's connect this back to 1 Peter 4:19. Peter's "*entrust* [your] souls to a faithful Creator" uses the same Greek word as Jesus's "I *commit* my spirit." Peter intentionally calls us to the pattern of Jesus's anguished faith on the cross.

God's high, sovereign providence in all things does take the panic out of life. Reasons for despair wash away. But grasp it rightly, and you'll never be matter-of-fact and coolly detached. God's purposes are to sanctify you. And his kind of sanctification aims for vibrant engagement with the real and immediate conditions of life, both the good and the bad. The contrasting expressions "All that is within me, joyously bless his name" (cf. Ps. 103:1) and "Hear my anguished cry for help" (cf. Ps. 102:1) both flow from sanctification. Christ fiercely opposes matter-of-fact detachment. It is the opposite of what he is like. God will teach you to experience life the way the Psalms express it.

My Story

During one season of my life I (unwillingly!) gained some enemies. I had to face repeated public and private insults. It stung. Being called names and lied about touches a deep nerve: "That's so wrong! That's completely unfair!"

What were these people like in their enmity? They were hostile. They mocked. They wanted nothing to do with me. They did not want to reconcile. In their eyes, I was anathema, an evildoer. In light of my apparent evil, they felt justified in their damning accusations.

One of the surprises that came with *becoming* a Christian was the discovery that there were people who hated me because of what I believed. One of the surprises of *growing* as a Christian was the discovery that some of the people who hated me were professing Christians. And one of the great compensatory *blessings* of growing as a Christian was realizing how perfectly the Psalms tune our hearts when we face malice and lies. We know David wrote his words for himself. We know that Jesus made these words his own. Yet we find that these words were also written for us. That is how Psalm 31 came to life in my experience.

I faced enemies, but I found a more serious enemy resident in my own heart. I became preoccupied, stressed, and distracted. The ways I was being mistreated got too much air time. The consuming evil was my craving to be vindicated, to be understood accurately, to be treated fairly. When taking a shower, or when awake at night, or when asked about the accusations, my mind would get busy constructing responses to the false and mocking things said about me. The temptation to return evil for evil takes many forms. Returning snark for snark was not my particular temptation (though such thoughts sometimes occurred). My trap was trying to answer false and offensive accusation by rehearsing defensive self-justification. I struggled off and on for months. I needed help.

And God helped. He did not let me drown in deep waters. He was with me to bless my troubles and sanctify my distress. He used many means of grace, and it took time, but here are the leading notes of how he did it.

It so happened that our church retreat that winter focused on finding the touch points where we needed God's hand and voice to work in our lives. As soon as this goal for the weekend was introduced, I knew that my wrongful reaction to wrong was the issue of the hour. I saw the wrong of attempting self-justification in the face of unfair condemnation. God's judgments are accurate, merciful, and decisive. I was fretting too much about someone else's judgmentalism. My preoccupation led to sins of omission when I was distracted rather than attentive to my family, friends, students, and colleagues. My preoccupation was driven by fear of man, pride, the desire to be understood, and love of a good reputation. Simply naming the issue brought a measure of perspective and purpose.

At the end of the first evening's talk, our pastor asked each of us to consider what passage of Scripture might speak words of life into the place where we were struggling. After some pondering, I chose the closing lines of Psalm 31:

How great is Your goodness,
Which You have stored up for those who fear You,
Which You have wrought for those who take refuge
    in You,
Before the sons of men!
You hide them in the secret place of Your presence from
    the conspiracies of man;
You keep them secretly in a shelter from the strife of
    tongues.
Blessed be the LORD,
For He has made marvelous His lovingkindness to me in a
    besieged city.

. . . .

Be strong and let your heart take courage,
All you who hope in the LORD. (Ps. 31:19–21, 24 NASB)

Those words *spoke.* They captivated me by their insight, intimacy, and vigor. They captured my experience of threat and what it was like to be besieged by hostile words. They breathed safety and goodness in the Lord's protective presence. The last line of the psalm called me to reenter life, family, and ministry energetically.

I delighted in this picture of how our God stores up and works good, and how he hides and shelters us within his goodness. "The strife of tongues" gave me a handle for what was coming at me. I repented of trying to act as defender of the realm of my reputation. The Lord forgives freely, and he made his loving-kindness marvelous to me. I let go of the desire to convince my attackers, forgave them, and resolved to seek peace

71

if an opportunity arose (though multiple efforts were rebuffed). That final charge—"Be strong, and let your heart take courage!"—stirred me like the skirl of bagpipes.

Verbal attacks, my sinful reactions, my heart's deviant motives, liberating Scripture, and a wise pastor combined to animate my processing, prayers, and coming to terms. I was significantly freed to set preoccupation aside and refocus on the people and tasks God had placed in front of me. The changes were not instantaneous but unfolded over several months.

One more person deserves honorable mention in the process. An older, wiser man played a crucial role in bringing all this home for me. He is a man in whom God's words dwell richly and then come forth savory, bright, timely, and alive. I hadn't known him very well before, but a long and wide-ranging conversation established our friendship. He helped me properly assess all the players in the situation. He affirmed that the accusations being made were baseless and that I should view such words as swallows that flit around and never land (Prov. 26:2). Yet he noted that enmity still hurts. People who bear false witness are likened to clubs, swords, and sharp arrows (Prov. 25:18); the victim of rash words feels stabbed with a sword (Prov. 12:18).

It turned out that he had known my accusers years earlier, that one of them had been excommunicated from a church for divisiveness, and that another was a loose cannon who had never joined a church. My friend had himself been publicly slandered by one of them. He reminded me that you can never make peace with a factious person (Titus 3:9–11). He encouraged me to leave it behind and move on, to love the people God had called me to love and do the things God had called me to do. Most of all, he reaffirmed and embodied the goodness and loving-kindness of our God; he reaffirmed and embodied that the Lord sympathizes with us in our afflictions; and he reaffirmed and embodied how the Lord's care is protective and constructive. As we talked, I thought about the second half of Proverbs 12:18, which he had mentioned: rash words stab, but "the tongue of the wise brings healing." *Thank you, my friend.*

Unfathomable things operate at the core of why and how we change and grow. An organic, dynamic, relational process—where every element is touched by God's presence, hand, and voice—eludes our ability to dissect, explain, script, or control. We are dealing with the ongoing work of the Potter who works in his clay in order to make us more potter-like in every way that is communicable to a creature. Infinite variations of multiple factors are at work. No two stories are the same. God himself is involved in it all. The process is never quantifiable. That said, in general terms, variants on five factors interweave in my story and in every story of how his grace works into the difficulties of our lives.

First, *God himself is the author of life*. He makes alive. He cares. He speaks. He shepherds. He initiates. He responds. He prunes. He disciplines. He animates. He strengthens. He protects. He forgives. He leads. He listens. We who are ignorant and wayward live in continual relationship to the One who knows all things and always engages with us. In the story I just told, he was working.

Second, *we humankind are doubly afflicted*. We struggle with countless sufferings and with the madness in our hearts.

We struggle because hard things come at us from outside and because dark things come from inside us. Our experience, both objectively and subjectively, cries out in need for intervening grace. In my story, I felt the pain of hostility and the pressure of lies. Then I struggled within the tangles of self-preoccupation and the impulse to vindicate myself.

Third, *God's Word brings light and mercy into darkness and deviance*. Through words, we learn the saving love of Father, Son, and Holy Spirit. It is according to these words that the Vinedresser, Shepherd, and Lifegiver rewrite the script of our lives. In my distress, Psalm 31 opened to me the secret place of his presence filled with goodness. His call to strength and courage was effective.

Fourth, *other people bring God's grace*. The church's public ministries and the personal ministries of wise people unite to communicate God's grace with a voice of firsthand experience, a loving heart, and a helping hand. For me, the context of teaching and directed reflection at the retreat was a significant means of grace. My friend's wise counsel consolidated many disparate strands.

Fifth, *we ourselves turn from darkness to light*. We ourselves take his words to heart. We entrust our very lives into God's hands. We act differently. In my story, I responded to his promise of good. I forgave my attacker and gave up attempts to justify myself. I redirected my time and energies where they belonged.

Making It Personal for You

What "category" of significant suffering have you been focusing on as you've been reading? Health problems and interpersonal hostility, as in my three stories thus far? Verbal, physical, or sexual violence? Money woes? Prejudice and put-downs because of your race, sex, faith, disability, or socioeconomic status, or some other bias that is socially embedded? The aftereffects of a moral failure? Some other hardship?

Just as I shifted from health afflictions to interpersonal affliction, is there a different woe in your life that God would have you face fruitfully? Bring the God of our hymn's third stanza into contact with your trouble. He will "sanctify to you your deepest distress."

6

MY LOVING PURPOSE IS
YOUR TRANSFORMATION

The fourth stanza of "How Firm a Foundation" makes God's purpose even more explicit. He designs your significant suffering for three reasons. He is revealing his abiding generosity toward you. He is removing all that is ungenerous in you. He is making you abidingly generous.

> When through fiery trials your pathway shall lie,
> my grace, all-sufficient, shall be your supply;
> the flame shall not hurt you; I only design
> your dross to consume and your gold to refine.

Our merciful Lord is with us to work out this purpose. The metaphor of fiery trials that cannot finally harm you comes from Isaiah 43:2. But this stanza's core promise arises from 1 Peter 1:6–9. Peter uses the metaphor of a smelting furnace. You are a mixed—mixed up!—creature. In God's hands, experiences of suffering purify you. His love works to take away what is wrong with you: your dross. The outcome is a growing love and joy toward God in Christ, as well as a more sincere love for others: your gold. Peter says that this is the fruit of faith, because you have never actually seen Jesus. But he becomes more and more real in the context of fiery trials. We will look first at the dross and then at the gold.

Your Dross to Consume

Most of the time, we are right to separate sufferings from sins. What you do is different from what happens to you. Your sins are bad things about you as a moral agent. Your sufferings are bad things that happen to you. Agent and victim are opposite in principle. And most of this book has naturally focused on the things that happen *to* you. As a new creation in Christ, you live in an essentially different relationship to your sufferings.

But it is worth noting that you, as new creation in Christ, also live in an essentially different relationship to your own sinfulness. Your sin now afflicts you. The dross of your blind spots and besetting sins no longer defines or delights you. The sin that indwells becomes a form of significant suffering. What you once instinctively loved now torments you.

What sins do you still wrestle with? Forgetting God and proceeding as if life centers on you? Obsessive religious scrupulosity that starves your humanity? Defensive and self-assertive pride? Laziness or drivenness, or an oscillation between both? Irritability, judgmentalism, and complaining? Immoral impulses and fantasies? Obsessive concern with money, food, or entertainment? Fear of what others think about you? Envy of good things that someone else enjoys? Shading truth into half-truths to manufacture your image? Speaking empty or even destructive words, rather than nourishing, constructive, and graceful wisdom?

These sins are endemic to everyday life. Perhaps you recognize the "seven deadly sins" (and a few extras) within that list of the mundane madness of our hearts! I can identify with each one, and I suspect you can too. Our Father loves us with mercies new every morning and more numerous than the hairs on our heads. He is good and he does good. He has chosen to love us. And we really do love him—as street children he has rescued and adopted. But our love is far from perfected. C. S. Lewis vividly captured our ongoing, widening, deepening struggle with all that needs God's redeeming mercies:

> Man's love for God, from the very nature of the case, must always be very largely, and must often be entirely, a Need-love. This is obvious when we implore forgiveness for our sins or support in our tribulations. But in the long run it is perhaps even more apparent in our growing—for it ought to be growing—awareness that our whole being by its very nature is one vast need; incomplete, preparatory, empty yet cluttered, crying out for Him who can untie things that are now knotted together and tie up things that are still dangling loose.[1]

Whether we find ourselves tied in knots or dangling at loose ends, God hears our cry. He says, "You are mine. So take heart. I will complete what I have begun."

The essential change in your relationship with God radically changes your relationship to remaining sinfulness. In Christ, in order to sin, you must lapse into temporary insanity, into forgetfulness. It is your worst cancer, your most crippling disability, your most treacherous enemy, your deepest distress. It is the single most destructive force impacting your life. Like nothing else in all creation, this threatens your life and well-being.

Saying that our sins afflict us like a madness is not to justify or excuse our derangement. Your sin is *your* sin. When you get your back up in an argument, when you vegetate in front of the TV, when you spin a fantasy world of romance or eroticism, when you grumble about the weather, when you obsess about your performance in the eyes of significant others, when you worry, nag, or gossip, *you* do these things. No evil twin, no hormone, no satanic agency, and no aspect of your upbringing can take credit or blame for the works of your flesh. You do it. You want to do it—but you don't *really* want to, when you come to your senses. And you do come to your senses. The conflicted dual consciousness of the Christian always lands on its feet, sooner or later. Yes, you drift off and commit sin. But you turn back to the Lord because you are more committed to him. And you are more committed to him because he is absolutely committed to you, and the new creation is already at work in you. Many psalms capture this tension between our proclivity to sin and our fidelity to our Redeemer from sin. They confess the dark vitality of indwelling sin while confessing love for the triumphant mercies and goodness of the Lord.[2]

In moments of sane self-knowledge, you view your dark tendencies as an affliction: "I am what I do not want to be. I do what I do not want to do. I feel what I do not want to feel. I think what I do not want to think. I want what I do not want to want." You know the inner contradiction: "I want to love God joyously, but meander in self-preoccupation. I want to love others freely, but lapse into lovelessness. I want to forgive, but brood in bitterness. I want to give to others, but find that I take from them or ignore them. I want to listen and learn, but find I am opinionated and narrow-minded. My biggest problem looks at me from the mirror."

But indwelling sin does not define you. It opposes you. It is an aberration, not an identity. Self-will is a living contradiction within you. So you look far beyond the mirror: "Lord Jesus, your love for me will get last say. You are merciful to me for *your* name's sake, for the sake of *your* own goodness, for the sake of *your* steadfast love and compassion (Psalm 25). When you think about me, you remember what *you* are like, and that is my exceeding joy. My indestructible hope is that you have turned your face toward me, and you will never turn away."

All the promises of our hymn apply to the significant suffering of indwelling evil, as well as to the evils that come at you from outside. You probably did not initially identify a pattern of indwelling sin as your most significant suffering. But put the two together. How does God use your known external trouble to reveal the sins he is working on internally? How do you know that he will deliver you from the sins that afflict you? He will consume your dross in the fire of his love for you.

81

Your Gold to Refine

What does your gold look like? The first thing to notice is that it's *your* gold. God has begun in you a good work of faith and love. Earlier I portrayed how faith thinks and speaks according to the intelligent passion of the Psalms. And that faith leads somewhere very, very good. Here we will examine two key aspects of the love that faith produces. The most remarkable good things that the planet has ever seen or will ever see can only come out in the context of suffering. We will look first at courageous endurance and then at wise love. The refiner's fire brings forth gold out of affliction.

1. *Grace teaches you courage.* When God says, "Fear not," his aim is not that you would just calm down and experience a relative absence of fear. He does not say, "Don't be afraid. Everything will turn out okay. So you can relax." Instead he says, "Don't be afraid. I am with you. So be strong and courageous." Do you hear the difference? The deep waters have *not* gone away. Troubles still pressure you. The opposite of fear is courage, not unruffled serenity. Fearlessness is courageous in the face of fearsome things. It carries on constructively in the midst of stress that doesn't feel good at all. Courage means more than freedom from anxious feelings. Endurance is a purposeful "abiding under" what is hard and painful, and considering others even when you don't feel good.

There are countless ways to simply lessen anxiety: vigorous exercise, getting all the facts, Prozac, cognitive behavioral therapy, finding the best possible doctor, yoga, a vacation in Bermuda, a glass of wine, getting some distance from the problem, finding support from fellow sufferers, throwing yourself into work. Some of these are fine in their place. But none of them will make you fearless in the face of trouble. None of them creates that resilient fruit of the Spirit called "endurance," which comes up repeatedly when the New Testament talks about God's purposes in suffering. None of the strategies for personal peace gives you the disposition and power to love another person considerately in the small choices of daily life. None of them gives you high joy in knowing that your entire life is a holy experiment as God's hands shape you into the image of his Son. None of them changes the way you suffer by embedding it in deeper meaning. None gives you a reason to persevere in fruitfulness through all your days, even if the scope of your obedience is constricted to your interactions with nurses at your bedside.

2. *Grace teaches you wise love.* In fact, fearless endurance is for the purpose of wise love. God is making you like Jesus in the hardships of real life. Jesus combines two qualities that rarely go together: true compassion and life-rearranging counsel. He intends to combine them in you. Some helpers care intensely but don't know what to say. They feel helpless compassion. They offer platitudes. They reinforce the self-pity and entitlement of the victimized. Other helpers dispense advice but don't enter the plight of sufferers. They serve up cold counsel. They become impatient when a sufferer is slow to change. They dismiss the significance of the affliction of the afflicted. Neither is able to really comfort or guide.

But when you've passed through your own fiery trials and found God to be true to what he says, you have real help to offer. You have firsthand experience of both his sustaining grace and his purposeful design. He has kept you through pain; he has reshaped you more into his image. You've found our entire hymn to be *true*. What you are experiencing from God, you can give away in increasing measure to others. You are learning both the tenderness and the clarity necessary to help sanctify another person's deepest distress.

Second Corinthians 1:4 says it best: "God . . . comforts us in all our affliction, so that we may be able to comfort those who are in any affliction, with the comfort with which we ourselves are comforted by God." That word "comfort" (or "encourage," in some translations) does not simply mean solace or inspiration. You take heart. You are strengthened. You experience God's transformative compassion, the perfect union of his kindness and candor. He speaks the truth in love so that you grow up to do the same.

Notice two things. First, the way God meets us in our need turns our faith and love into generalizable skills that meet others in their need. The comfort you receive from God in your *particular* affliction becomes helpful to others in *any* affliction. A hymn written nearly 250 years ago can help us in our afflictions because it speaks relevantly about the encouragement someone else received. Second, remember that God's uses people as part of how he encourages. Second Corinthians 1:4 is not only about drawing encouragement from gospel truths in the privacy of your mind! Reaffirming your love for someone who is forgiven brings comfort with a personal touch (2 Cor. 2:7–8). Paul was comforted because the Corinthians were in his heart and their hearts were open to him. He was encouraged because Titus came and told him about this. He was encouraged because Titus had been comforted. He was comforted because the Corinthians' earnest faith was obvious (2 Cor. 7:4–16). The correspondence between God's touch and the human touch is one of the deep delights of our Christian faith.

God's personal tenderness, unchangeable truth, and high purposes are united so that he simultaneously accomplishes seemingly contradictory things. He profoundly comforts us as sufferers, strengthening us for endurance. He mercifully challenges us as sinners, humbling us with our ongoing need for the blood of the Lamb. He powerfully changes us as his sons and daughters, making us fearless and wise to help other sufferers, other sinners, other sons and daughters. There is inevitably an aloneness in suffering because no one can fully enter another's experience. Each person knows "the affliction of his own heart" (1 Kings 8:38; cf. Prov. 14:10). God ensures that human aid will never substitute for the Lord, who alone comes fully near. But we can bear each other's burdens with love, and we can counsel each other with truth. The give-and-take of wise love is one of life's most significant joys.

My Story

When I was fifty years old and had been a Christian for twenty-five years, I needed open-heart surgery. Recovery after surgery had its agonizing moments. But the long-term sequelae were far worse than the short-term pain. The next five and a half years were the hardest of my life.

From 2000 to 2006, I inhabited a body that did not work. I had no resilience. I did not bounce back from normal fatigue. I was on a downward spiral of shattering weariness and increasing disability, unable to sustain normal social life and ministry life. I liken those years of cumulative losses to living through a slow-motion building collapse. Only family, a handful of friendships, and writing remained fruitful. I had to count the cost of every social interaction. Teaching was an ordeal—I could just make it through a semester. I love counseling, but it was too wearing—and I had to stop.

And, through it all, God met me and changed me for the good. Change sometimes occurs in a decisive moment. In previous chapters, my first two stories involved a relatively dramatic turn, something that took place within a day or just a few minutes. The third story was of a slower process—I came to terms with hostility over a period of months, with several significant spurts.

Much of how we grow is a matter of slow-forming habits—the accretion of new patterns of thinking, attitude, and response. Much of our growth happens subliminally, the way a child grows. Like any skill, wisdom includes definable, explicit things learned, moments we can describe. But like any skill, wisdom also involves tacit, implicit, caught-not-taught learning. There are ways I have grown that I could never quantify, that I do not even see. God retains the right to work in ways beyond our comprehension. Because learning how to live is the most complex skill imaginable, the struggle will not cease until I have faced the last enemy and see the face of God.

My experience over five and a half years was the genesis of the book you are reading. It took its basic shape and tone toward the end of those years—at a time when the cause of my fatigue was still mysterious, and when I had no earthly hope that my condition would ever improve. My life was withering. This is why what I write is premised on holding in tension three complementary realities.

- We face certain inescapable afflictions that will prove insoluble until tears are wiped away when we see Christ face-to-face.
- Many afflictions are momentary, or last for a season, and then we are restored.
- God is at work in us, both when our sufferings have a remedy and when they do not.

In the long run, after those five-plus dark years, I was surprisingly restored to health by the discovery and treatment of a sleep disorder. But this is not a story of medical cure (joyous as that was). It is a story about the ongoing cure of a soul. How did God work?

First came the suffering itself. Amid cascading losses and troubles, all familiar habits and assumptions were tossed up into the air like confetti. I became like a man in his eighties, not his fifties. Life had changed, with no explanation and no solution. God works in and through suffering. Suffering is a means of grace, according to Scripture. My faith and love had to grow up—as I always have to grow up—*again*.

Second, a handful of wise, godly friends played a very significant role. Some were going through analogous experiences (dying of cancer, or disabled by chronic pain or chronic fatigue). They understood. Their compassion and insight were not retrospective. It was not, "Been there, done that." We were in this together: "I'm here, doing this." Other friends knew me well enough to translate their sympathy into helping me take realistic action. They helped me to plan and to act within marked limitations. I needed both the tenderness and the realism. Both are aspects of practical wisdom. Both incarnate Jesus Christ. My family played a different role. They did not counsel me. They simply cared, and I cared for them. These were years where I paid a steep price for social interaction. My family's tenderness meant the world to me.

Third, the wisdom of saints whose race finished long ago played a significant role. Public worship sustained and instructed me—even when I had to duck out before the benediction so I would not be worn down by interaction. I have always loved wise, well-crafted hymns that invite me to think as well as sing. (Hence a hymn gave us this book's framework!) But I had never realized how many hymns (like the Psalms) inhabit suffering. They seek and find our Savior in the midst of hurt and perplexity.

For example, Katharina von Schlegel's "Be Still, My Soul" gives honest voice to her anguish and bafflement. She also gives expression to her hope and joy, including her reasons for hope amid grief. The Lord is on your side, even in this. He is your best—your heavenly—friend, who will not bereave you. He rules this storm, too. He soothes dark emotions. He will restore to you love's purest joys. Von Schlegel gives all these gifts to us. I look forward to meeting her, and I will thank her for helping me.

Fourth, I cannot express how often God's creation proved sustaining, refreshing, and sanctifying. In all seasons and weathers I went outside and walked. I noticed the flight of a goldfinch, snow on the stones in the brook, a field of white dogwoods in bloom, a thunderstorm rising in the west, maple leaves like fire in the fall. I was repeatedly drawn out onto a bigger stage than my troubles. I would pray my need and my gratitude out loud while walking. Theologians who limit the means of grace to overtly redemptive religious practices miss something about the God who speaks without words in the theater of his creation.

Fifth, the God who speaks and acts animates all these means of grace. God met me with his words and his Spirit—through preaching, through the Lord's Supper, through the informal counsel of friends, through my own reflecting on Scripture, through creation, through suffering. I heard God's voice of truth and sought him, and found him. As familiar words engaged my current experience, those words took on meanings and resonances I could not have imagined. I needed God's grace in new ways. How many times had I read the Psalms? But now it was like I was reading them for the first time. My faith needed to find expression in new ways. Obedience had to take new forms. It was like hearing God's promises and commands speaking a new language—different, yet familiar, long believed, but now coming at life from unexpected angles. Here are some of the passages that inhabited my heart and mind, and repeatedly met me. These are elemental revelations. They link my weakness and need to God's mercies, protection, and strength.

Matthew 5:3–10. If the Sermon on the Mount is Jesus's keynote address, then the Beatitudes are the keynote of his keynote. The seeds of the whole are in these eight beatitudes. In the first four, blessing bonds to weakness as we depend on God: honest neediness, sorrow at all wrong, submission within God's will, and longing for all to be made right. In the second four, blessing bonds to strength as we move out into the world: active generosity, purity of purpose, constructive engagement, and courageous endurance. Jesus lived this unusual interplay of weakness and strength, of dependency and action. This is what it looks like to be truly human. *Holy Spirit, make me into these things.*

Psalm 103. I can't begin to say how often and how profoundly this psalm has befriended and renewed me. It describes my need and draws forth my faith. It takes me by the hand into needing, trusting, and worshiping my Father. It enables me to love others who share in the iniquity, frailty, dependency, and mortality of the human condition. Psalm 103 is a rough charcoal sketch anticipating the living color of Ephesians 1–3. "All the good things he does" (Ps. 103:2, lit. trans.) is the prequel to "every spiritual blessing" (Eph. 1:3) that we find specified and fulfilled in Christ. *Bless the Lord, O my soul, and do not forget.*

Psalm 119. The way I had been taught about this psalm, it was a treatise on the nature of Scripture and an exhortation to Bible study. The way I have come to learn and live this psalm, it shows me how to talk with God and what to talk about. It expresses how personal honesty is redeemed from the odor of self-centeredness. Scripture, prayer, and suffering meet.

> *I will keep your statutes;*
> *do not utterly forsake me! (119:8)*

2 Corinthians 1:4 and Hebrews 5:2–3. My firsthand experience does not terminate in me. It is transmuted so that I become able to deal gently and helpfully with others in their struggles. These passages portray a most curious and wonderful dynamic. My particular troubles—mastered by the God of mercies and comfort—equip me "to comfort those who are in any affliction" (2 Cor. 1:4). My sins and weaknesses—dealt with honestly before the Lord, who gives mercy and grace to help in time of need—equip me to minister well even to "the ignorant and wayward" (Heb. 5:2). *Jesus, teach me to counsel others the way you counsel me.*

———

I'll stop there. The bookshelves in my home could not contain all that could be written about those hardest years. In suffering, I learned to need mercy. From suffering, I learned to give mercy. The living faith that embraces Christ is formed in the crucible of weakness. The courage to carry on and the strong love that cares well for others are formed in the crucible of struggle.

How did I change? I was changed because God never let me go and he shines in all that's fair. I was changed because Scripture spoke many words of God's mercy, protection, strength,

91

and will. I was changed because many friends bore me up. I was changed because I had to walk through darkness and destruction, within the uncertainty of no explanations and no solutions. I was changed because I repeatedly turned outward in faith and love, reversing my inward-turning tendency.

Making It Personal for You

We twenty-first-century people are hasty folk. We like things to happen fast. We want problems to have quick solutions so we can move on to something else. But God has made our souls to work on agricultural time and child-rearing time. You can't rush the process that grows a good tomato to eat in late summer, still warm from the sun. You can't rush the process that nurtures a child who grows up into a fine human being. The problems of suffering don't have quick "solutions." Afflictions are part of the process by which God nurtures his children to grow up into fine human beings. Take some time to wrestle through these questions and texts:

What does it mean that your significant suffering plays an intrinsic role in how you will know the love of God poured into your heart? (Rom. 5:3–5)

_____

_____

What does it mean that your significant suffering plays an intrinsic role in how you will know joy inexpressible and full of glory? (1 Pet. 1:3–9)

_____

_____

What does it mean that your significant suffering plays an intrinsic role in how you will know the peace of Jesus Christ? (John 16:33)

_____

_____

What does it mean that your significant suffering plays an intrinsic role in how you will become deep and wise? (James 1:2–5)

_____

_____

What does it mean that your significant suffering plays an intrinsic role in how you will learn to truly help other people who suffer? (2 Cor. 1:4)

_____

_____

Love, joy, peace, wisdom—and the ability to make a difference. That's what it means to grow up into a fine human being. That's what it means for your dross to be consumed and your gold to be refined. The way you go "through fiery trials" along your pathway makes all the difference.

7

I WILL PROVE MY LOVE TO
THE END OF YOUR LIFE

All that we've looked at so far continues even into old age. This is remarkable. The author of "How Firm a Foundation" showed great sensitivity to the human condition by addressing the challenge of growing old:

> E'en down to old age all my people shall prove
> my sovereign, eternal, unchangeable love;
> and when hoary hairs shall their temples adorn,
> like lambs they shall still in my bosom be borne.

Down to Old Age

Readers already "adorned" with gray or white hair—big fans of Psalm 71!—will immediately appreciate why a hymn for sufferers must tackle aging. Most people in their seventies and beyond say something along this line: "Growing old is not for the fainthearted." God is not intimidated by the things that make us quail. He encourages the fainthearted, and in doing so he teaches us how to encourage each other.

Every single reader who lives a long life will experience a landslide of losses and disabilities. Live long enough and you may outlive everyone you love: parents, friends, spouse—even children and, perhaps, grandchildren. You will outlive your usefulness in the workplace and other productive arenas. You may outlive your money. You may outlive your relevance and no longer be part of what's happening. You may outlive your health as every bodily system breaks down. You may outlive your ability to walk, your toilet training, your ability to feed yourself; your memory and—toward the end—your ability to put thoughts together, to relate to others the way you wish you could, and even to remember who you are. Should you live long enough, you may lose every earthly good. And then you certainly will lose your life. The last enemy still routinely kills us.

Our hymn mentions only the outward indicators: the accumulating years, the white hairs. But those allusions tip you off to a story of weakness, hardship, and finally the impending loss of life itself. It is in this context that God gently and persistently promises to prove his "sovereign, eternal, unchangeable love" to his aged people: "like lambs they shall still in my bosom be borne." He tenderly carries the helpless—and what a lovely inversion of the metaphor, that the elderly become like newborn lambs who must be carried. Old age mirrors, in reverse, the helplessness and limitations of infancy.

A dear friend had experienced many losses in her life. She

recently faced one more: a disfiguring facial surgery for cancer. She put her grief plaintively, "I didn't expect the scarring after the bandages came off. It's upsetting to look in the mirror. It's one more loss. And I feel so much uncertainty about whether the cancer will return. Then there's the loss of people, the isolation, the loss of human society, the parts of life in which I can no longer participate." She is a woman of articulate faith. She is honest about the pain of loss. But her God speaks the final, decisive word about her: "I will carry you and never let you go." That is perhaps the deepest comfort communicated by this hymn's way of communicating God's voice. He gets first say, and he gets last say. So everything in the middle—about which he expects us to have lots to say!—is anchored in sovereign, eternal, unchangeable love.

Like Lambs with the Shepherd

Amid the pain of loss, God teaches us whom to trust, what to trust, and what to say. Think back through the central promise that anchors each stanza in this wise, pastoral hymn: "I am with you. I am with you. I am with you." Each stanza reiterates essentially the same thing, giving us different details, unpacking fresh implications, supplying us with fresh metaphors to evoke a different nuance of God's inexhaustible riches of presence, wisdom, and love.

Psalm 23:4 has provided more comfort to more suffering and dying people than any other passage of Scripture:

> When I walk through the valley of the shadow of death,
>   I will fear no evil,
> because you are with me. (my trans.)

Through our entire hymn, God has been telling us that same truth from his direction. This allows the faith of verse 4 to say, "You are with me." Faith listens well, and gives what it trusts back to God.

I bring this up here because of the other details in Psalm 23:4–5. The route home to where the Lord lives passes through deep darkness, and we face many evils and many enemies. Like a sheep stalked by wolves, David lived much of his life under specific death threats. Like all of us, he lived knowing that death awaits. This applies powerfully to the hardships of aging. Death is coming nearer. Aging casts numerous specific shadows of approaching death: sickness, losses, weakness, helplessness, futility. In fact, if you are willing to think about it, whether you are young or old, *every* form of significant suffering, *every* evil, leaves something of the bitter taste of death in your mouth. It serves us well to think about it. Psalm 90:12 anchors wisdom in the willingness to face reality:

> So teach us to number our days
>   that we may get a heart of wisdom.

Is it depressing to think about it? No. It is sobering, of course. But reckoning well with the limit on your days is how you learn to live well. People who find it depressing to consider their limits have not reckoned with Jesus Christ. In reality, life will get last say. Life and joy will defeat death and despair.

The psalmist's "walk[ing] through . . . the shadow of death" is not simply an evocative metaphor, and "fear[ing] no evil" is not a vague generality (Ps. 23:4). The shadow and evil are person specific: they are your significant sufferings. Your need of God's grace to reach into your sufferings is more than theoretical. In affliction, you immediately feel your need. A shadow reaches toward you. It covers you. Its inner logic whispers or shouts of death. And God says, "I am here with you."

Can you honestly say, "I fear no evil"? Can you say that in terms of the specific evils and hardships of your life?

It all depends on whether you hear the God who gives you reasons to say it. If the God of life is in fact *with* you, carrying you as a newborn lamb, you can become fearless in any suffering. In the ups and downs, the painful struggles of a lifetime, this is the destination toward which you struggle. And if God pledges his absolute fidelity to you, if indestructible love will see you through to a good end, then you will be able to walk a very hard road.

And you will *have* to walk a very hard road. Death sends out many messengers along the way, even to the very young. But if you listen to your Shepherd's voice, you will become fearless. If you listen, you will endure. If you listen, you will fight the good fight in the most terrible of wars. If you listen, you will know that you need to be rescued. You will know that you need to be carried into the battle, and carried through the battle, and finally carried from the battlefield. If you listen to the Good Shepherd, you will live.

My Story

My mother died in 2015 after three hard years of steep decline. She was ninety-four. Vascular dementia is a tough foe. Strokes progressively destroyed her capacity for language and self-awareness. They left her increasingly confused and disoriented.

And during those same years, my mother suffered maddening and irremediable pain from shingles that settled in and around her left eye, cheek, temple, and forehead.

These withering losses of extreme old age are the opposite of normal child development, with its succession of flourishing gains. One difficulty both for Mom and for us was that her limitations were a moving target. Her location on the ability–inability scale was unpredictable. She would sometimes briefly stabilize, but then she would inevitably drift, slide, or plunge, always in the direction of inability. At the same time, her increasing limitations were robbing her of the capacity to adapt to her limitations. Growing old is not for the fainthearted. Caring for the elderly is not for the fainthearted. But, older or younger, we are all fainthearted.

God met Mom with genuine comfort, but he certainly did not make everything all better. As a Christian, right up to the end she was responsive to a word of promise from Scripture—eventually reduced to a single phrase, and even that paraphrased for simplicity. Frequently, that phrase was some variant on "Mom, you are not alone. Jesus is with you." She welcomed being prayed for—and that, too, was eventually reduced to a couple of short, simple sentences using concrete, one-syllable words. She welcomed a familiar hymn and did her best to sing along, even after her language abilities were significantly compromised. She welcomed our presence—the human touch was part of how God cared for and carried his lamb in her weakness.

God walked with my mother, though the bright spots became smaller and the darkness became greater. It is no surprise that Mom's faith, humility, and love remained incomplete. Our besetting struggles with sin do not disappear. They morph into new forms under new conditions of temptation. Her church had been weak in nurturing that dynamic of the Psalms and Beatitudes that teaches us to willingly recognize need, which naturally opens a door to asking for help from God and others. Most of us have a streak of "I can do it myself. I don't want help." That stubbornness and refusal to ask for help complicated her downward slide into helplessness. It complicated her difficulties in recognizing limitations. So she remained imperfect. But that, too, was under the mercy.

When Mom was in confusion or distress, both the human touch of her children and simple reminders of Christ's love often—not always—brought a calming presence. When I said goodbye to her for the last time, she could not understand the concept that I was leaving. (She lived in Hawaii; we in Philadelphia). At this point she was living only in the present moment, like a child. Her emotional responsiveness had been significantly dulled and flattened. But God gave us an inexpressibly tender moment. Cheek to cheek, I said, "I love you, Mom." She said, with remarkable alertness, clarity, and vigor, "I love you, too, son." I can still hear her voice say those words, and I weep again to tell the story. There were some joyous, even humorous moments, even in the final stages. One Sunday afternoon a few months before she died, my brother and sister played familiar hymns from YouTube and sang along with her. Mom so awakened to the singing that my brother commented afterward, "I think Mom probably gained six more months of life!"

As I've thought back, I've wondered whether Mom lost the capacity to "self-generate" faith in her last year. She had lost self-awareness. Did she also lose the ability to reflect consciously on her God, to hold some truth in her mind, and then articulate an inward response to him? In the end, was her faith only a response to a loved one's presentation of a Word, hymn, or prayer—a reflex animated by the Spirit's presence in her otherwise inarticulate heart? I don't know, but I suspect she lost the capacity for reflection and a self-initiated response.

"When I am weak, then I am strong" (2 Cor. 12:10). In her final decline she embodied incapacity to the nth degree. She had become one of those weakest members of the body who are indispensable to the rest, in whose sufferings all suffer together, whose protection and nurture is a revelation of the corporate sanctification of the body of Christ (1 Cor. 12:22–26). Consciously articulate faith is a desirable gift. But I suspect that its loss is no barrier to the love of a Savior whose kingdom is premised on choosing what is foolish and weak to shame the worldly wise and presumptuously strong.

Mom's life and death were both a triumph of Christ's grace and a vale of tears. Katharina von Schlegel put it well:

Be still my soul: when change and tears are past,
all safe and blessed we shall meet at last.

Making It Personal for You

Psalm 90:1–11 reflects on the Lord's eternity and on the significance of our mortality. We sin; we live under his wrath; we die. Yet this Lord is our dwelling place and our hope. The next line turns toward him and makes a unique request:

So teach us to number our days
    that we may get a heart of wisdom. (90:12).

Would you make that request of God personal: "Teach me to number my days that I may get a heart of wisdom." How does God answer such a request?

_____

_____

You will die on some future day. You know your birthday, but you will not know your deathday until it arrives. What does your impending mortality mean to you? Most people simply dodge the subject and live in relentless denial. But God wants us to think about it. It is the only sure thing in life. Death is your final enemy. Death is the most significant, decisive suffering you will ever face. It awaits you in the future.

But God's grace is at work in your suffering—in the past, currently, and, most significantly, in the future. He himself is awaiting you in the future—beyond your death. Like a lamb, even in the nth degree of helplessness, even in your dying and death, you will still be carried to his house in his arms.

How can you know this? God's grace has been revealed in what he has already done with your inevitable death. You sin; you live under his wrath; you die. The Son of God, without sin, came under wrath and he died—in your place. And he was raised. This same Jesus Christ is alive, and you are alive in him. His Father is your Father and has joined you to his Son. Ask his Spirit to open your eyes to know "the immeasurable greatness of his power toward us who believe, according to the working of his great might that he worked in Christ when he raised him from the dead and seated him at his right hand" (Eph. 1:19–20). Given the inevitability of our dying, and the dire reasons why, the death and resurrection of Jesus Christ and the sending of the Holy Spirit form the most significant sequence of events in all history. It meant the killing of the author of life (Acts 3:15), the committing of the sin of sins, the coming of the day of judgment—and the sacrifice of the Lamb of God. And what happened next is on the order of the creation of the universe: God raised him from the dead (Acts 3:15) by the power of the Holy Spirit. And he sends his life-giving Spirit.

And when God awakened you to Christ and made you one with him, he did something else on the order of the creation of the universe.

> God, who said, "Let light shine out of darkness," has shone in our hearts to give the light of the knowledge of the glory of God in the face of Jesus Christ.
>
> But we have this treasure in jars of clay, to show that the surpassing power belongs to God and not to us. We are afflicted in every way, but not crushed; perplexed, but not driven to despair; persecuted, but not forsaken; struck down, but not destroyed; always carrying in the body the death of Jesus, so that the life of Jesus may also be manifested in our bodies. . . .
>
> . . . This light momentary affliction is preparing for us an eternal weight of glory beyond all comparison. (2 Cor. 4:6–10, 17)

Surpassing power, glory, and life are already working within you. Yet isn't it striking how current afflictions, troubles, sufferings, and even death are so tightly interwoven with the present activity of this glory? Immortality will speak the final word—but not yet. Christ rewrites the script of your life so that your death will not get last say on your life—but you will die on the way to life. He will walk with you—but you will walk through the valley of death on the way to where he lives. Resurrection is the center point of the gospel. Resurrection is what the gift of the Holy Spirit is about, uniting you to the Savior of the world. Resurrection is the reason that life will triumph in the end. Resurrection is the reason your life is not in vain.

Psalm 90:12–17 ends with a barrage of requests: "Teach us to number our days." "Return, O LORD!" "Establish the work of our hands" (90:12, 13, 17). Do read it all, and read it slowly.

Take to heart how the resurrection of Jesus Christ, the gift of the Spirit, our salvation, and the return of the King fulfill every request. The fulfillment begins with the resurrection. The curse is reversed. And if you know that the work of your hands is going to be established, then "my beloved brothers, be steadfast, immovable, always abounding in the work of the Lord, knowing that in the Lord your labor is not in vain" (1 Cor. 15:58).

8

I WILL NEVER FAIL YOU

We face many kinds of suffering, many enemies of our welfare. The last stanza of "How Firm a Foundation" identifies our ultimate enemy. A predator is looking for you. A roaring lion is on the prowl. Who will prevail?

> The soul that on Jesus has leaned for repose,
> I will not, I will not desert to his foes;
> that soul, though all hell should endeavor to shake,
> I'll never, no never, no never forsake.

The Final Enemy

At the beginning of this book, you selected some significant suffering in your life. You have held that in view as we have worked through our hymn, stanza by stanza.

But we've also been pushing the envelope and broadening the battle. In the previous chapter we focused on suffering at the hands of "the last enemy," death. In the chapter before that we talked about "the enemy within," how our sinfulness becomes a form of affliction. This final stanza pushes the envelope one more time. You have foes from hell. You face "the Enemy." The fact that you will die is not an impersonal datum. It registers the personal animosity of a killer. A Lord of Darkness is father to both sin and death. He personifies every aspect of the evils that come at us and the evils that come from within us.

When speaking of hellish foes that come after you, our hymn writer (like the Bible) is talking about reality—not the horror and fantasy genres in books, films, and video games. Ordinary, everyday life under the shadow of death is lived under the power of the Evil One. White hairs and birthday candles testify that a predator is coming soon. Satan is both the accuser and murderer of sinners. He holds the power of death (Heb. 2:14). He willingly conceals his workaday identity behind veneers of marketable horror, fantasy, and superstition. He gives the illusion that there nothing more to evil than meets the eye. He thrives when people *do* believe in him and picture a bogeyman. He thrives when people *don't* believe in him and instead dismiss him as a figment of overactive imaginations. The Evil One conceals himself in the fog of war. So unsuspecting people don't notice that he's in the mortality business, however it happens.

In calling out the powers of hell, our hymn writer (again like the Bible) is talking about all-pervasive reality—not lurid tales of Satan worship. He means garden-variety sin, unbelief, and self-will spun out into ten thousand forms. He means garden-variety suffering, affliction, pain, and loss. The fair and honest wage paid for ordinary sin is ordinary death (Rom. 6:23). The Evil One is the liar and tempter who works skillfully in and with the facts of sin. He is the murderer and torturer who works skillfully in and with the facts of suffering. It matters little to him whether or not people even believe he exists. He willingly conceals his real malignancy behind both wild tales and skepticism. So unsuspecting people don't notice that he's in the unbelief business, whatever form it takes.

You suffer in a world in which your immediate significant sufferings point to deeper, darker, deadlier things. The enemy within, the final enemy, and the Enemy—all three significantly afflict every one of us. They characterize the human condition. "The whole world lies *in* the evil one" (1 John 5:19, lit. trans.). We inhabit a slave world. A dark world. A death world.

But you suffer in a world in which all dark, deadly things exist within an even deeper design and calling. The drama of evil occasions the revelation of good, the deeper drama of the gospel. God's holy justice and sacrificial love unfold on the stage of darkness. He will bring all enemies to final justice. He has shown you and me wholly unmerited mercy. When we were helpless, when we were ungodly, when we were sinners, when we were enemies, Christ died for us. You are now free. You are light in the Lord. You live. "We are *of* God. . . . We are *in* Him who is true, *in* His Son, Jesus Christ. This is the true God and eternal life" (1 John 5:19–20 NASB).

If you have "leaned for repose" on Jesus, you will live. Repose here does not mean a restful state of peace and tranquility. It's the old original meaning: to rely entirely, to depend, to actively place the weight of your life on Jesus. Put your entire faith, confidence, and trust in him.

> Trust in the LORD with all your heart,
>> and do not lean on your own understanding.
> In all your ways acknowledge him,
>> and he will make straight your paths. (Prov. 3:5–6)

A Final Promise

This final stanza of our hymn aims to make you free and fearless, no matter what you have faced, what you now face, what you will face. *I will never forsake you*—God is willing to say it until you get it! The final line of the hymn sends us out with another of the Bible's core promises. In fact, it completes a quartet of two promises and two commands that God frequently links: "I am with you. Don't be afraid. Be strong and courageous. I will never forsake you."[1] We've discussed the first promise and the two commands in previous chapters. Here one final promise gets last say.

There is a particular appropriateness to closing with *I will never forsake you*. Sufferers feel apprehension about the future, for good reason. Some evils will not go away. The serious enemies we've considered in the past few chapters can never be comprehended, managed, or controlled. Shadows multiply and darken. The night is coming. And so this word of comfort looks to the future. It speaks right into our temptation to fear and dismay.

Notice how God's words press into you and lift your heart. The hymn has unfolded in a double crescendo. Our awareness of suffering, pain, weakness, and danger has steadily intensified. But with that, our awareness of God's powerful love at work has steadily intensified as well. Sin, misery, and death abound. Grace, joy, and life abound all the more. Mercy will have final say.

But we easily quail. We *feel* the force of things that undo us and would unglue us. They shake us up. They immediately hurt. Is God's saving voice mere words? Is what the Bible says really so? What if the dreaded x, y, or z actually happens? The hymn writer knows our vulnerability to dismay.

I'll never, no never, no never forsake.
I'll never, no never, no never forsake.

If you've ever sung this hymn with your brothers and sisters, these last lines come out fiercely triumphant.

In the pages of the Bible, God explicitly promises, "I will not forsake you" (see, e.g., Josh. 1:5). Once you know to look for it, you see that he says the same truth in a hundred other ways, too. "God is faithful" and "His steadfast love endures forever" and "The Lord is my refuge" are variations on a theme. What God says for himself, his spokesmen often proclaim about him, *He will not forsake you* (see, e.g., Deut. 31:6, 8). So with good reason his children cry out to him in their troubles and distresses, *Don't forsake me!* Again, hearing, we believe and speak. Scripture gives many particular examples of this dynamic. Are you elderly, suffering the weakness, pain, disability, and losses of aging? *Don't abandon me!* (Ps. 71:9, 18). Do you feel lonely and vulnerable as you face powerful interpersonal hostility, bereft of anyone who can protect you? *Don't desert me!* (Ps. 27:9–10). Do you feel dismayed that God has every reason to give up on you because of your sins? *Don't give up on me!* (Ps. 119:8). Are you doubly dismayed, both because of your sins and because of the hostilities of others? *Don't let me go!* (Ps. 38:17–21).

Our hymn takes God's simple "I will not" and says it ten times in a row: "I will never, no, never, no, never—never, no, never, no, never forsake you." Far more than a mere doubling, this is a promise to the power of ten. It is pastoral wisdom, helping us to hear the fierceness and triumph of God's loving-kindness. You will never be abandoned. You will never be alone. He will never give up on you.

Never forget this. Never forget. Never, never, never forget that he will not forsake you.

My Story

Worship, sermons, and fellowship have a cumulative effect. I have been a believer in Jesus Christ for more than forty years. I have heard many sermons. I have sung many hymns, carols, and songs. I have taken the Lord's Supper many times. I have been in many conversations and prayed many prayers. But I don't vividly remember many particular sermons or worship services or times of prayer. The vast majority of them blend together in a cluster of memories, like impressions from one's childhood merging the experiences of many years.

But I do vividly remember a few moments. In the late 1970s I heard a sermon on Romans 8:26 that I've never forgotten. The text was "The Spirit helps us in our weakness." I remember the exact point: "Notice that our weakness is singular, not plural. Paul does not say weaknesses, plural, as if you could make a list. He says weakness, singular, as our defining characteristic. We *are* weakness. We are weakness because of sinfulness. We are weakness because of fragility and mortality. We need our Father to set his love on us. We need Jesus Christ to rescue us. We need the Spirit to help us and make us alive. And he does."

Psalm 40 makes a similar point, with more vivid detail. David summarizes his view of God this way:

> As for you, O LORD, you will not hold back
> your compassions from me.
> Your steadfast love and your faithfulness will
> daily guard me! (40:11, my trans.)

And David summarizes his view of himself this way:

> As for me, I am poor and needy,
> but the Lord takes thought for me.
> You are my help and my deliverer;
> do not delay, O my God! (40:17)

"As for you," "as for me." That captures elemental reality. It is the dual truth that rewrites the script of your life.

Making It Personal for You

We have come far. Let me suggest that you read our entire hymn slowly. Then respond back to the God who speaks to you. Sing it to *Adeste Fideles*—the same tune as "O Come, All Ye Faithful." Take it to heart. Pray. Trust. Give thanks.

How firm a foundation, you saints of the Lord,
is laid for your faith in his excellent Word!
What more can he say than to you he has said,
to you who for refuge to Jesus have fled?

"Fear not, I am with you, O be not dismayed;
for I am your God, and will still give you aid;
I'll strengthen you, help you, and cause you to stand,
upheld by my righteous, omnipotent hand.

"When through the deep waters I call you to go,
the rivers of sorrow shall not overflow;
for I will be with you, your troubles to bless,
and sanctify to you your deepest distress.

"When through fiery trials your pathway shall lie,
my grace, all-sufficient, shall be your supply;
the flame shall not hurt you; I only design
your dross to consume and your gold to refine.

"E'en down to old age all my people shall prove
my sovereign, eternal, unchangeable love;
and when hoary hairs shall their temples adorn,
like lambs they shall still in my bosom be borne.

"The soul that on Jesus has leaned for repose,
I will not, I will not desert to his foes;
that soul, though all hell should endeavor to shake,
I'll never, no never, no never forsake."

Our God means what he says, and he does what he says he
will do.

CODA

So often the initial reaction to painful suffering is "Why me? Why this? Why now? Why?" You've now heard God speaking with you through the truths of "How Firm a Foundation." The real God says all these wonderful things and does everything he says. He comes for you, in the flesh, in Christ, into suffering, on your behalf. He does not offer advice and perspective from afar; he steps into your significant suffering. He will see you through and work with you the whole way. He will carry you even in the most difficult situations. This reality changes the questions that rise up from your heart. That inward-turning "Why me?" quiets down, lifts its eyes, and begins to look around.

You turn outward and a new and wonderful question forms. "Why you? Why you, Lord of life? Why would you enter this world of evils? Why would you go through loss, weakness, hardship, sorrow, and death? Why would you do this for me, of all people? But you did. You did this for the joy set before you. You did this for love. You did this showing the glory of God in the face of Jesus Christ."

As that deeper question sinks home, you become joyously

sane. The universe is no longer supremely about you. Yet you are not irrelevant. God's story makes you just the right size—neither too big nor too small. Everything counts and everyone matters, but the scale changes to something that makes much more sense. You face hard things. But you have already received something better, which can never be taken away. And that better something will continue to work out the whole journey long.

Why you? The question generates a heartfelt response. "Bless the Lord, O my soul, and do not forget any of the good things he does, who pardons all your iniquities and heals all your diseases, who redeems your life from the pit, who crowns you with loving-kindness and compassions, who satisfies you with good things as your adornment, so that your youth is renewed like the eagle. Thank you, my Father." You are able to give true voice to a *thank you* amid all that is truly wrong, because all sins and all sufferings have now come under his loving-kindness.

Finally, you are prepared to pose—and to mean—an almost unimaginable question: "Why *not* me? Why *not* this? Why *not* now?" If in some way, your faith might serve as a three-watt night light in a very dark world, *why not me?* If your suffering shows forth the Savior of the world, *why not me?* If you have the privilege of filling up the sufferings of Christ? If he sanctifies to you your deepest distress? If you fear no evil? If he bears you in his arms? If your weakness demonstrates the power of God to save us from all that is wrong? If your honest struggle shows other strugglers how to land on their feet? If your life becomes a source of hope for others? *Why not me?*

Of course, you don't want to suffer, but you've become willing—like your Savior, who said, "If it is possible, let this cup pass from Me; yet not as I will, but as You will" (Matt. 26:39 NASB). Like him, your loud cries and tears will in fact be heard by the One who saves from death. Like him, you will learn obedience through what you suffer. Like him, you will sympathize with the weaknesses of others. Like him, you will deal gently with the ignorant and wayward. Like him, you will display faith to a faithless world, hope to a hopeless world, love to a loveless world, life to a dying world. If all that God promises only comes true, then *why not me?*

NOTES

Introduction

1. C. S. Lewis, *The Problem of Pain* (1940; repr., San Francisco: Harper-SanFrancisco, 2001), 91.
2. This book is based in part on David Powlison, "God's Grace and Your Sufferings," in *Suffering and the Sovereignty of God*, ed. John Piper and Justin Taylor (Wheaton, IL: Crossway, 2006), 145–73.

Chapter 2. How Firm a Foundation

1. This version of the lyrics, updated to more modern language, is from the *Trinity Hymnal*, rev. ed. (Philadelphia: Great Commission Publications, 1990), no. 94. (The *Trinity Hymnal* credits Rippon's *Selection of Hymns*, 1787; alt.) It can be sung to several well-known tunes. My favorite is *Adeste Fideles* (also the tune of "O Come, All Ye Faithful"), which doubles the last line of each stanza.
2. Traditional Irish hymn, sixth or eighth century, trans. Eleanor Hull, 1912.
3. John Newton, 1779.
4. Attributed to John Francis Wade, 1751, trans. Frederick Oakeley, 1841.
5. Katharina von Schlegel, 1752, trans. Jane Borthwick, 1855.
6. Charles Wesley, 1742.
7. J. Wilbur Chapman, 1910.
8. Dan McCartney, *Why Does It Have to Hurt? The Meaning of Christian Suffering* (Phillipsburg, NJ: P&R, 1998).

Chapter 4. I Am with You

1. J. I. Packer, in Packer and Mark Dever, *In My Place Condemned He Stood: Celebrating the Glory of the Atonement* (Wheaton, IL: Crossway, 2007), 113.

Chapter 6. My Loving Purpose Is Your Transformation

1. C. S. Lewis, *The Four Loves* (London: Harcourt Brace, 1991), 3.
2. Most people associate psalms of confession (e.g., Psalms 32, 38, 51) with this theme. But Psalm 119 most vividly captures the dual consciousness that lands on its feet. See "Suffering and Psalm 119," in David Powlison, *Speaking Truth in Love* (Greensboro, NC: New Growth, 2005), 11–31. Psalm 25 and Romans 6–8 are also filled with this holy ambivalence which lands on God's side of the struggle.

Chapter 8. I Will Never Fail You

1. See Deut. 31:6, 8; Josh. 1:5; 1 Chron. 28:20.

GENERAL INDEX

General Index

faith
  endurance and dependency of,
    20–21
  listens well, 98
fatalism, 63
fear, 47–48, 50, 57, 110
fearlessness, 82–83
"fear not," 82
fiery trials, 77–78, 83, 93
filling up the sufferings of Christ,
    117
fool/foolish, 37, 45

gifts, become identity, 40
God
  as author of life, 73
  compassion of, 84
  as Creator, 64–68
  encourages through other
    people, 84
  faithfulness of, 111
  goodness of, 14
  nearness of, in our affliction, 52
  at our side, 62
  promises of, in our fear and
    dismay, 50–57
  sovereignty of, 62–68
    mechanical view, 66
  speaks through afflictions, 14
  voice of, in hymns, 26–28
  will never forsake us, 110–12
gold, refining of, 82
good gifts from God's hand, 13
grace
  abounding in suffering, 111
  in death and dying, 103–4
  fits our need, 20
  from other people, 74
  sufficiency of, 41–42
  teaches courage, 82–83
  teaches wise love, 83–85
  works in hardship, 14–16

grief, 53
growth, through slow-forming
    habits, 86

half-kindness, 55
hardship, 44, 49
Holy Spirit, communicates God's
    words, presence, and love, 28
"How Firm a Foundation"
    (hymn), 23–25, 29, 113–14,
    115
  first stanza, 33
  second stanza, 47
  third stanza, 61
  fourth stanza, 77
  fifth stanza, 95
  sixth stanza, 107
hymns, 88
  speak to suffering, 25
  sung to the Lord, 29–30
  sung to the self, 30

Immanuel, 52
immortality, 105
incurvatus in se, 50–51
indwelling sin, 78–81
isolation, 48

Jesus Christ
  betrayed by friends, 53
  leaning on, 109–10
  poured out heart on the cross,
    67–68
  resurrection of, 104, 105
  suffering of, 49, 115–16
"Jesus, What a Friend for Sin-
    ners!" (hymn), 29–30
Job
  afflictions of, 11–12
  isolation of, 52–53
  temporal joys of, 13–14
Jordan River, 61

SCRIPTURE INDEX

How Does Sanctification Work?

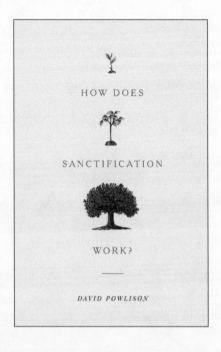

Weaving together personal stories, biblical exposition, and theological reflection, David Powlison shows that the process of sanctification is personal and organic—not a one-size-fits-all formula.

"David's is a voice of sound, biblical wisdom in the midst of much confusion. If you are looking for a book on sanctification that is profoundly personal, biblically balanced, and deeply relevant, then this is it."

Heath Lambert, Associate Pastor, First Baptist Church of Jacksonville; Executive Director, Association of Certified Biblical Counselors

For more information, visit crossway.org.